PAUL TODAY

PAUL TODAY

CHALLENGING READINGS OF ACTS AND THE EPISTLES

ESSENTIAL INQUIRIES, VOLUME 1

STEPHEN W. NEED

COWLEY PUBLICATIONS

Lanham, Chicago, New York, Toronto, and Plymouth, UK

Published by Cowley Publications
An imprint of Rowman & Littlefield Publishers, Inc.
A wholly owned subsidary of
The Rowman & Littlefield Publishing Group, Inc.
4501 Forbes Boulevard, Suite 200
Lanham, MD 20706

Estover Road
Plymouth PL6 7PY
United Kingdom

Distributed by National Book Network

Library of Congress Cataloging-in-Publication Data

Need, Stephen W. (Stephen William), 1957–
    Paul today : challenging readings of Acts and the Epistles /
Stephen W. Need.
        p. cm. — (Essential inquiries ; v. 1)
    Includes bibliographical references and index.
    ISBN-13: 978-1-56101-296-1 (pbk. : alk. paper)
    ISBN-10: 1-56101-296-3 (pbk. : alk. paper)
    1. Paul, the Apostle, Saint. 2. Bible. N.T. Acts—Criticism, interpretation,
etc. 3. Bible. N.T. Epistles—Criticism, interpretation, etc. I. Title. II. Series.
    BS2506.3.N44 2007
    227'.06—dc22   2007013753

Printed in the United States of America.

∞™ The paper used in this publication meets the minimum requirements of
American National Standard for Information Sciences—Permanence of
Paper for Printed Library Materials, ANSI/NISO Z39.48-1992.

For Philip and David

CONTENTS

INTRODUCTION

*P*aul Today: Challenging Readings of Acts and the Epistles and its companion volume, *The Gospels Today: Challenging Readings of John, Mark, Luke & Matthew*, have arisen out of my teaching New Testament studies in various institutions in England and to groups in the Holy Land, Greece, and Turkey over a period of more than twenty-five years. Both volumes are designed to enable students and other interested readers to get a quick overview of a number of issues or problems in the areas concerned. Together, the chapters present a profile or silhouette of issues that arise in studying a text or theme from Paul or the Gospels. They show the range of concerns that arise from a particular New Testament text or theme to give you, the reader, a working knowledge of what's at stake in trying to understand and interpret a particular text or problem, and, I hope, to stimulate you to do further reading on topics and texts that interest you particularly. But there is more than this. Taken together, the chapters demonstrate ways of approaching New Testament texts and issues. For example, they show how historical and theological questions play a part in understanding a text; how exegetical issues can make serious differences; how matters relating to ancient Judaism and the Greco-Roman world have a place in interpreting these texts for us today; how questions of language are crucial; how archaeology can illumine a text; and how patristic and other interpretations of texts might have obscured an author's intentions. Together the chapters show how a number of academic disciplines and concerns are appropriate and indeed necessary to the interpretation of New Testament texts and themes. It is in this sense of providing overviews of important texts and issues in New Testament studies that the two volumes are introductory; they are not introductions to the New Testament or to their respective areas as such.

This first volume focuses on St. Paul. I discuss and challenge popular interpretations of familiar Pauline texts and themes in presenting overviews of important controversies and debates. Thus, the task of constructing a biography of Paul is complex, for although some of the well-known features of his life as portrayed in the Acts of the Apostles turn out to be trustworthy, others do not. The relation between Paul and Jesus is not easy to discern, and it is important to steer a path between too much confidence and too much skepticism when trying to find connections between the two. The role of the city of Ephesus in Paul's life and theology, and in later Paulinism, turns out to be more significant than is usually thought; Paul's attitudes to marriage and to slavery are much more positive when the historical and social context of his first letter to the Corinthians is taken into account. A discussion of the problems Paul faced over food that had been sacrificed to idols shows the importance of conscience and the eucharist in his theology. Women were much more prominent in Paul's life than has traditionally been thought, and his attitude to them and their ministry look very different when the specific context of his words is taken fully into account. Parts of Paul's letters have been used in the many recent debates about homosexuality, but it is clear that Paul himself was arguing in a very different context and viewed the matter in a very different way from those engaged in contemporary discussions of this subject. There has been a major revolution in Pauline studies in the last half-century, producing a completely "new look" on Paul and his theology that is still not widely known. A close study of the christology of Philippians 2:6–11 and Colossians 1:15–20 and their contexts in the letters concerned shows how christology, ethics, and ecclesiology were all fundamentally related in Paul's thinking. The traditional understanding of the "fall" and of "original sin" arising out of Romans 5:12–21 can now be seen to have been thoroughly misleading. And the notion of "justification by faith," popularly associated with Paul, can now be seen to have arisen out of later interpretations of his theology, rather than out of a close reading of his own words. So in all the chapters, I debate and reframe familiar interpretations of Paul through this kind of challenge and critique.

Most of the issues I deal with in these chapters are very well known to scholars working on Paul but remain largely unknown outside academic circles. Many people who think they know Paul well remain unaware of the critical problems discussed in college New Testament classes. And many who might be interested would perhaps be at a loss to know how or where to begin to deal with such critical problems if they were faced with them. For example, looking closely at what Paul originally wrote to the Corinthians in the light of both the original background and of modern critical methods can be an exciting and informative adventure for general readers, both Christian believers and skeptics alike.

So these chapters make constructive, critical approaches to Paul available to a wider circle of interested readers. Whatever your background, you will be able to see the sorts of problems raised by serious study of Paul. Whether you are a student wanting a quick overview of a subject in Pauline studies for an assignment or an examination, a preacher preparing a sermon, or simply a reader interested in how critical and theological concerns can come together in healthy and constructive interpretations of Pauline texts and themes, these eleven essays on Paul will be of interest to you.

Each chapter is complete in itself and can be read independent of the others, and the chapters can be read in any order.

While the views expressed in the essays are my own and do not represent any institution or organization, there are many persons for whose help with this manuscript I am grateful. I would especially like to thank Professor Leslie Houlden for reading an early draft of this book, and my wife, Jill Dampier, for checking the final manuscript. Any remaining errors are my own responsibility.

Stephen W. Need
Jerusalem
June 2006

ONE

A PORTRAIT OF PAUL
PAINTING A PICTURE
OF THE APOSTLE TO
THE GENTILES

What manner of man was St. Paul? For many people the "apostle to the Gentiles" is a mystery and an enigma defying all definition. In the popular imagination he is a negative figure whose writings forbid many of the good things of life. In scholarly circles he is notoriously difficult to understand, and remarkably different accounts of his life and theology have been written. Since his own time, Paul has been interpreted and reinterpreted by admirers and critics alike, and from the second century onwards some of the greatest theologians of the Christian church have radically misinterpreted him. And there are those today who claim that Paul is the real founder of Christianity.

It is, of course, the mark of greatness to defy narrow definition, and Paul's elusiveness is in some ways a sign of his stature and importance. But the portraits of Paul that have come down to us from historians, theologians, and artists are so frequently misleading that there is a need to get an overview of Paul the man if we are ever to appreciate his significance fully.

So what do we really know about Paul? Where was he born, and what were the formative influences on his life? What difference did his famous Damascus Road experience make? And are the well-known traditions of his three missionary journeys, his tent-making, and his study with Gamaliel in Jerusalem, really true? It should, of course, be easier to find the historical Paul than the historical Jesus, for we have a number of letters written by him. But Paul's letters actually give us very little biographical material, and what we do know about his life comes to us largely from the Acts of the Apostles written later by Luke.

In trying to find the "real Paul," therefore, we must weigh the evidence carefully and systematically. The concern in this chapter is with what we can know about Paul the man; how best to go about finding this out; and what a responsible portrait of him might look like in the end. I shall, therefore, first, look at the sources available for painting a portrait of Paul; second, consider what the sources actually tell us; and third, offer a portrait of the man behind the texts as far as he can be found.

The Nature and Date of the Sources

To get at what we really know about Paul and what a portrait of his life might look like, we first have to consider the nature and date of the sources available to us. Two sources form the basis of any understanding of Paul's life: his own letters and Luke's Acts of the Apostles. The relation between these two sources is complex and has been the subject of much debate and disagreement especially in the last half-century, mainly to do with which of these two sources is the more reliable and which we choose to believe when a conflict appears. Traditionally, the Acts of the Apostles has formed the basis of research into Paul's life, and most of the well-known information about Paul, for example his birth in Tarsus and his "missionary journeys," comes from Acts. So scholars have usually followed Acts and then filled in any further detail from Paul's own writings.

Recently, however, it has been suggested that it makes more sense to follow Paul's own letters as the key source and to treat

Acts as secondary and as having its own literary, doctrinal, and other motivations, following Paul more closely when there is disagreement. The likely date of the two sources of course affects such a decision. Obviously Paul's letters come from his own lifetime and from the situations in which he himself lived and worked in the 40s and 50s of the first century CE. Luke's Acts of the Apostles, on the other hand, comes from about half a century later, toward the end of the first century.

On the whole, then, it does seem more sensible to rely on Paul's own writings first of all and to acknowledge that Luke wrote Acts later with his own specific theological and literary perspectives. However, we must be careful with the so-called Pauline writings themselves, for out of the thirteen New Testament letters that bear Paul's name, probably only eight are actually by him. Most scholars are now agreed that 1 Thessalonians; 1 and 2 Corinthians; Romans; Galatians; Philippians; Colossians (disputed); and Philemon are genuinely Pauline. On grounds of differences in style, vocabulary, and content it is now usually thought that the remaining five New Testament letters that bear Paul's name are not actually by him. They are: Ephesians (disputed); 1 and 2 Timothy and Titus (the Pastoral Epistles); and 2 Thessalonians. In the light of all this, it is wise to base this investigation into what we know about Paul on the authentic Pauline letters and on the Acts of the Apostles. Apocryphal works on Paul from later centuries, such as the *Acts of Paul*, cannot be used as serious historical sources for a portrait of Paul.

Paul in the Acts of the Apostles

On the grounds that the Acts of the Apostles has fed the Christian imagination about Paul for centuries, we shall begin by observing just what the main features of the traditional portrait are. We shall then be able to see Paul's letters in that light and see how little of the Acts material is actually in them. This does not mean that what Acts says and what Paul says are invariably incompatible, but simply that the author of Acts has his own perspective and paints his portrait of Paul in a particular way. What, then, are the key features of Luke's portrayal of Paul in Acts?

Acts is not only about Paul; it is about other apostles as well, especially Peter. Paul only comes into real prominence in the second half of Acts. However, he is by far the dominant apostle in the narrative. His first appearance is at the death of Stephen (7:58) when he is called Saul and is clearly Jewish. Luke tells us that he is from Tarsus in Cilicia, which is apparently his birthplace (cf. 9:11; 22:3). He is persecuting followers of Jesus and is on his way to Damascus in pursuit of them (9:1f.). Paul's dramatic encounter with Jesus on the road to Damascus changes his whole perception of Jesus, and he is baptized in Damascus and begins his work there for Jesus. This Damascus Road event is related three times in Acts with varying detail and purpose (9:1–25; 22:1–16; 26:12–18).

After the first account, Paul becomes much more central in Acts and from chapter 13 to 28 is predominant. In later chapters we learn that he was educated in Jerusalem under Rabbi Gamaliel (22:3); that he was a Pharisee (23:6); and that he had Roman citizenship (22:27).

Then, of course, there are the three great "missionary journeys" (13–14; 15:40–18:22; 18:23–21:17). Paul begins in Syrian Antioch and takes the Gospel of Christ out first to Jews and then to Gentiles in a series of expanding circles, across the Mediterranean to Asia Minor and Macedonia and back again. In the journeys, Paul visits synagogues, is rejected, and then turns to the Gentiles (9:15; 18:6). He founds communities, and after the three journeys he returns to Jerusalem and is arrested. Next he is taken to Caesarea and tried under Felix, Festus, and Agrippa (24–26). He then makes his final journey to Rome (Acts 27) and is shipwrecked on Malta on the way (28:1). In Rome he stays for two years preaching the Gospel at his own expense.

The narrative of Acts ends there, and it is later texts that tell us of Paul's martyrdom in Rome. This portrait of Paul from Acts is well known, but how reliable is it and how does it relate to what Paul himself tells us?

It is clear that in Acts, Luke presents Paul's story as part of the "success story" of the early Christian mission stretching out from the Jewish world beginning in Jerusalem into the Gentile world and culminating in Rome. Jerusalem is central for Luke, and Paul's life revolves around the city and the church there. Paul's relations with the Jerusalem church are smooth, successful, and unifying, and Paul the energetic traveler returns there on several occasions.

However, almost every feature of Luke's presentation of Paul in Acts can be challenged in the light of Paul's own letters. For a start, the Paul of Acts never writes a single letter! Nor does Luke call him an apostle. Furthermore, Paul is a powerful orator whose dramatic speeches form a dynamic element in preaching the Gospel and in coming into conflict with the Jerusalem church. Yet from Paul's own letters we learn that he was not a powerful speaker at all (2 Cor. 10:10; 11:6). These are just some indicators that there are a number of serious differences of emphasis between Acts and Paul's own letters.

A Portrait of Paul

It is remarkable that most of the well-known details about Paul's life come from Acts and do not appear in Paul's own letters. From Paul himself, for example, we learn nothing of his birth in Tarsus; of his tentmaking; of his education under Gamaliel; of his missionary journeys; of his journey to Rome; or even of his Damascus Road experience as such. This does not mean that Acts is not trustworthy, however, and we shall now look at these features in turn and in the light of Paul's own letters and other considerations to see what the likelihood of their historicity is. We cannot simply decide every issue on the probable historicity of Acts overall. There are four main areas of interest in painting a historically credible portrait of Paul.

First, Paul's birth, background, education, and occupation. Although Paul does not himself tell us of his birth in Tarsus, there is no reason why this should be doubted and there is no obvious reason why it should have been invented. In the fourth century a tradition that Paul was born in Gischala (modern Jish) in Upper Galilee was known to St. Jerome, but there is no other evidence for this and Tarsus remains the more likely option. In any case, Paul most probably grew up in Tarsus. Situated in modern south-central Turkey, Tarsus was the capital city of Cilicia at the time of Paul. It was renowned for its high educational standards and competed in this respect with other major cities such as Athens and Alexandria. By Paul's day the region had been thoroughly Hellenized as well as Romanized and the Greek education system would have operated in Tarsus. Paul would have attended the ordinary school and then the Gymnasium. There would have been a good deal of solid education including rhetoric, letter-writing, and classics, in addition to physical education. Paul eventually wrote his letters in Greek and obviously commanded the language well.

As he was also Jewish, he would have received an education in the synagogue system, whatever that might have been in his place at that time. There is little knowledge of Jewish education in Tarsus at the time of Paul, but it would obviously have involved learning Hebrew and knowing the Torah. In fact, we know at least something about this from Paul's own hand. In what is probably the most reliable biographical passage we have from Paul, he tells us that he was "circumcised on the eighth day, of the people of Israel, of the tribe of Benjamin, a Hebrew born of Hebrews; as to the law a Pharisee, as to zeal a persecutor of the church, as to righteousness under the law, blameless" (Phil. 3:5–6). He is, therefore, thoroughly Jewish; he knows the Torah well, and belongs to the Pharisees. Although our knowledge of the Pharisees before 70 CE is limited, they were a powerful group committed to the interpretation of the Torah.

Another consideration here is the detail in Acts that Paul was educated in Jerusalem under Gamaliel (22:3). This is never mentioned by Paul himself and has attracted a great deal of discussion. Was Paul actually educated in his youth in Jerusalem rather than Tarsus? How strange that Paul himself never mentions being taught by one of the greatest rabbis of the first century. It is possible that Luke's detail is correct; Paul's silence on the matter certainly does not falsify the tradition. However, the detail fits so well with Luke's portrayal of Paul linking him up with Jerusalem that one must be wary. Also, Gamaliel was a thoroughly liberal figure and a key leader in the school of Hillel. Depending on how Paul himself is interpreted, it is often thought that Paul's own views would have conflicted seriously with those of Gamaliel and that it is therefore unlikely he spent long studying with him. There is a great deal of uncertainty here, but it is likely that Luke has included this feature in order to add color to his portrait of Paul.

From Acts we learn of two other elements that are significant in terms of Paul's social status. These are the detail that he was a Roman citizen (Acts 16:37–38; 22:25–29; cf. 25:6–12) and also that he was a tentmaker (18:3). Again, Paul never mentions his Roman citizenship himself and could well have done so on occasion, especially when he was in danger of execution (2 Cor. 1:8–9). It is certainly possible that he inherited Roman citizenship in Tarsus or inherited it from his parents. It is perhaps more likely, however, that like many Jews of his day, Paul simply belonged to the Jewish *politeuma*, a status less than that of citizen but which gave people some social autonomy. Paul's own silence on his citizenship and the fact that it is again well within the ideals of Luke's portrayal of Paul as a Roman suggest good reason to be wary here.

A final feature to consider is that Paul was a tentmaker. Again this comes from the pen of Luke, but there seems to be no reason why Luke or anyone else should have invented it. In fact, Cilicia where Tarsus was located was famous for its work with goat hair. The term used by Luke (*skenopoios*) is usually thought to be much broader than simply "tentmaker" and probably included leatherwork generally and the construction of awnings among other things. Paul himself, of course, is of the opinion that those who preach the Gospel should get their living by the gospel (1 Cor. 9:14; cf. Matt. 10:10; Luke 10:7–8) but there is no specific reason otherwise to doubt that Paul had a trade in his earlier life.

Finally, then, we can say that Paul would have had a good education in the Greco-Roman and Jewish worlds. He was a highly educated individual whose general cultural pedigree is clear, even if some of the details related in Acts are doubtful.

Second, Paul's life-changing experience. Sometime shortly after 30 CE Paul underwent a dramatic experience that changed his entire life. It also changed his perception of God, of Jesus, of those who followed Jesus, and of just about everything else too. According to Acts he was on his way to Damascus from Jerusalem in order to persecute followers of Jesus. In an incident that is related three times in Acts with interesting variations (Acts 9, 22, and 26), Paul is on his way to Damascus and Jesus appears to him. This is a dramatic "one off" incident after which Paul sees things in a totally new way. It is very strange that Paul himself never mentions this incident as such in his own letters, although some commentators take Galatians 1:11–17 to be a reference to it. In Galatians Paul writes of a major turnaround that looks more like one of the Jewish prophetic callings of the Hebrew Bible (Gal. 1:15) than a dramatic "conversion." Paul sees himself as set apart before he was born for the task that God wanted him to do. It is then three years before he begins to act.

The relation between the Acts accounts and what Paul says in Galatians is unclear. Some commentators see them as basically the same event, the Acts accounts being stylized narrative versions of the more complex religious experience recounted by Paul himself; others are less happy with this solution. More important than the type of event that took place is its significance in Paul's life. It was a radical change in perception. The incident in Acts has, of course, been painted by artists for centuries and has become known as "the conversion of St. Paul." Whatever else it was, however, it was not a conversion from one religion to another. It is quite unhelpful to think of Christianity as a separate religion at this stage, and in any case we know from Paul's own writings that he still saw himself as essentially Jewish after his Damascus experience. For Paul, what had happened near Damascus was something that helped him see the real significance of being Jewish, but now in Christ. Paul had not left the religion of his childhood, but he did experience a radical reorientation of his entire understanding of what that meant. This event, whether we follow Acts or Galatians, comprises the single most important event in Paul's life; it was the event that established him as the "apostle to the Gentiles."

Third, Paul the traveler and letter writer. After Paul's Damascus experience, a new phase of his life began, a phase in which his zeal was now directed in favor of Christ and the church instead of against them. It was at this stage that Paul's traveling and letter-writing began. It is interesting to note here a striking difference between Acts and Paul's own letters. It is in this main part of his life that the Paul of Acts makes his three "missionary journeys" around Asia Minor and Macedonia. However, these so-called missionary journeys are never mentioned by Paul himself. It is clear that Paul traveled and we have his letters to specific communities to prove it. But Paul doesn't mention three separate journeys. Did he ever make these journeys? Or are they features of Luke's narrative presentation of Paul in Acts? It is more likely that they are Lukan motifs and that Paul traveled all over the place haphazardly, not in increasing concentric circles as portrayed in Acts. Paul obviously did make journeys to Jerusalem and to a variety of cities in the Mediterranean world, founding communities or visiting communities founded by others. In this case it is simply a matter of following Paul rather than Acts. In this way, the Acts portrait is modified but not substantially changed. In relation to Paul's letter-writing, the picture needs similar adjustments. Paul obviously wrote letters, even if we disagree about which ones. But in Acts, Paul never writes a single letter. He is a speaker instead. Overall, it seems that Paul wrote letters and traveled, even though the Acts portrayal is not quite complete in itself and needs Paul's own letters to complement it.

Finally, Paul the Pastor. It is important, if we are to try to paint a reliable portrait of Paul, to try to appreciate what he was like as a pastor. In order to do this it is important to see how he dealt with the people and problems he faced. Too often, Paul has been portrayed as a systematic thinker whose Epistle to the Romans reflects the substance of his thinking and who was crystal clear on major issues. Others have claimed that Paul was a thoroughly confused man with many axes to grind and many prejudices to work through. His own words in 1 Corinthians, "I have become all things to all men" (9:22) have often been quoted to illustrate this. In reality neither of these two impressions does justice to the picture of Paul that emerges from a serious reading of his letters. Broadly speaking, from the letters the sense is of one who does not "have all the answers" to questions with which he is confronted. On the contrary, although his life has been radically changed, he struggles with issues that arise and deals with them afresh in each context. First Corinthians is the best example of a letter that shows Paul dealing in context with issues relating to splits in the community, sexual immorality, marriage and divorce, worship in the churches, the place of women in worship, and matters relating to the resurrection of Jesus. In each case, Paul does not simply give out preconceived answers but struggles with issues happening right there and then. He preaches the Gospel of Christ crucified and struggles to discern the way forward now that he and the community are "in Christ." He certainly can say different things to different people in different contexts, but this usually reflects the different needs of the different communities he deals with. Overall, the picture is of one who struggles with the message of the cross in and for each different context.

So what would a reasonable, historically responsible portrait of Paul actually look like? We have seen that there is a problem with the sources at our disposal for Paul's life. The Acts of the Apostles, which contains more biographical material relating to Paul than any other document, was written several decades after Paul's lifetime by Luke and is quite clearly a narrative account heavily influenced by Luke's own theological perspective. This does not mean that Acts cannot be taken seriously, but it must be approached with caution. Of the letters attributed to Paul, only the ones actually known to be by him can be used, although there is actually very little biographical material in them.

Given this situation with the sources, our investigation must proceed with care. We have only been able to look at some of the material here, but an important profile has emerged. There seems no good reason to doubt that Paul was born in Tarsus in Cilicia and that he was educated in three cultures: Hellenistic, Jewish, and Roman. He wrote and presumably spoke Greek and some Hebrew. He belonged to the Pharisees. His profession is likely to have been a worker with goat hair and leather. The tradition that he was educated in Jerusalem under Gamaliel, however, seems less likely, as does the tradition that he was a Roman citizen. It is clear that as a young man Paul persecuted Christians in the area of Damascus and underwent a dramatic experience of Christ that changed his life completely. This experience has been interpreted in many different ways, but it is misleading to think of it as a "conversion." It was, rather, a change in perception of God and his purposes, of Jesus, and of Paul's own mission. After the dramatic experience, the zeal with which Paul had persecuted the church was channeled in its favor as he felt called on a mission to preach the Gospel of Jesus Christ to the Gentiles. Paul now began his letter-writing and traveling, and although the picture of three missionary journeys in Acts needs modifying, it is clear that Paul did travel across Asia Minor, Macedonia, and the Mediterranean world, founding and visiting Christian communities and preaching the Gospel to them. Paul's Gospel message was lived out in his role as a pastor as he struggled to discern God's will for the communities in the many different circumstances in which he found himself. Overall, Paul must have been an earthy, energetic figure, alive with the Gospel and a love of his people; he was highly educated and well traveled, a writer and preacher whose radical experience of God in Christ had changed his life and had driven him to share his good news with others.

TWO

PAUL AND JESUS
A NEW TESTAMENT
CONUNDRUM

The problem of the relation between Paul of Tarsus and Jesus of Nazareth often seems virtually insoluble to students of the New Testament. There are so many unanswered questions that it is impossible to form a clear picture. Did Paul and Jesus ever meet? Did Paul encounter Jesus in Jerusalem or elsewhere when he was persecuting Christians? What did Paul really know about Jesus? And why is there hardly anything about Jesus' life and teaching in Paul's letters? Even more important, does Paul portray Jesus' message and significance correctly in his theology? Is he really faithful to Jesus' message of the kingdom of God and the love of neighbor?

The problem of trying to sort out the relation between Paul and Jesus historically is made worse by the fact that because there are so many interpretations of both men, it is hard to know where to begin. The general problem is made even more difficult by the nature of the sources at our disposal. Jesus lived and died before Paul wrote his letters, but all the evidence about him comes from the Gospels, which were written after Paul. Also, perhaps because Paul's life was dramatically changed by Jesus, Paul is far more interested in Jesus' significance for faith than with simple historical facts about him. More broadly, although Jesus has traditionally been seen as the founding figure of Christianity and Paul its first great theologian, some recent writers have claimed that Paul obscured the message of Jesus and is the real founder of Christianity as we now know it.

So it seems more important than ever to get the relationship between Jesus and Paul sorted out. But however necessary the task might be, the conundrum remains. The aim in this chapter is modest: it is simply to provide an overview of what Paul seems to know about the historical Jesus and his message and attitudes, basing the investigation on Paul's letters and to a lesser degree, the Acts of the Apostles. Our approach is threefold: first, to consider material in Paul's letters that either concerns the historical Jesus or echoes material in the Gospels; second, to examine the attitudes, as far as is possible, of Paul and Jesus on the question of the Jewish law; and third, to investigate what can be known about the relationship between Jesus and Paul from Acts.

Jesus in the Letters of Paul

The conundrum of the relationship between Paul and Jesus lies in the nature of the sources. Obviously Jesus lived before Paul's letters were written, but all our evidence for Jesus comes from a time after Paul's letters. This means that there is an inherent circularity in the quest for the relation between Jesus and Paul: we look for the historical Jesus in Paul but we have no pre-Pauline evidence about Jesus upon which to base our search. The Gospels were written in the second half of the first century after Paul's letters were completed, and although they may contain material that goes back to a time before Paul, it is impossible to know clearly when or whether this is the case. In fact, it is sometimes easier to find the influence of Paul in the Gospels than the presence of the historical Jesus in Paul's letters. In spite of the inherent difficulties, however, the task is still worth carrying out in order to try to gauge what the relation between the two men might be. The task is mostly a matter of making educated guesses based on the available material rather than one of dealing with straightforward factual knowledge leading in one direction or another. In this task, one must be careful at all times to avoid both too much confidence and too much skepticism. So we begin with the simple question, "What does Paul know about the historical Jesus?" The concern here is not with Paul's spiritual or confessional knowledge of Jesus as found in his life-changing Damascus experience, but with what he knows factually about the historical figure of Jesus of Nazareth, who according to the Gospels was born in Bethlehem, preached the kingdom of God in Galilee, taught in parables, performed miracles, went to Jerusalem and died on a Roman cross, and was seen again by his disciples after his death.

It is well known, in fact, that Paul has nothing to say about most of this. He does, of course, mention Jesus' death on a cross repeatedly and certainly sees this as a historical fact, but his concern is with its significance for his theology. We are given no passion narrative such as dominates the endings of the four Gospels. The nearest Paul gets to such a narrative is, perhaps, his accounts of the last supper (1 Cor. 11:23–26) and of the resurrection (1 Cor. 15). Otherwise there are no narrative accounts of anything. Paul doesn't seem to know of Jesus' birth in Bethlehem as it is told in Matthew and Luke; he never includes a parable of Jesus from the synoptic Gospels, and, what is even more remarkable, never alludes to one in his own teaching. Paul never includes narratives of Jesus' miracles or of events such as the Transfiguration which are so central to the synoptic understanding of Jesus. However, these silences are only part of the picture. There are at least three other types of material to consider.

First, Paul refers to "tradition" (1 Cor. 11:2; 2 Thess. 2:15) and to receiving things from "tradition" and to "handing them on," in his narratives of the Last Supper (1 Cor. 11:23) and on the resurrection (1 Cor. 15:3–4). These traditions are widely thought to constitute serious connections at least with the earliest Jerusalem church even if not with Jesus himself. The language of "handing on" here is technical terminology reflecting a serious concept of tradition. Second, if Paul does not give us narratives of Jesus' life, what does he tell us about Jesus? What would we know about Jesus if we only had the letters of Paul? We would know of Christ's connection to Abraham and David (Gal. 3:16; Rom. 1:3); that he was born under the law (Gal. 4:4); that he had a meal with his disciples the night before he died (1 Cor. 11:23f.); that he was crucified (cf. Gal. 3:1; 6:14); that the Jews were involved with his death (1 Thess. 2:15); and that he was buried and raised from the dead (1 Cor. 15:4).

Paul is also familiar with some of the apostles (Peter, James, and John—Gal. 2:9); he knows that some of them are married (1 Cor. 9:5); and that James is Jesus' brother (Gal. 1:19).

Third, there is the question of whether Paul knew particular sayings of Jesus. In 1 Thessalonians 4:15 Paul refers to having a "word of the Lord" relating to the end of time, and there are a number of significant overlaps between things Paul says in his letters and things Jesus says in the Gospels. For example, Paul encourages the Christians in Rome to bless their persecutors and repay no one evil for evil (Rom. 12:14, 17; cf. 1 Cor. 4:12–13). There are similar exhortations in Matthew 5:44–48 and Luke 6:27–30. Paul says that love is the fulfilling of the Law (Rom. 13:8–10; cf. Deut. 6:4 and Lev. 19:18), which is paralleled in Matthew 22:35–40. In Galatians 6:2 Paul says that bearing one another's burdens fulfills the law of Christ, and this is paralleled by the material on a brother who sins against someone in Matthew 18:15 (cf. 1 Cor. 9:21). References to the "coming crisis" might also be noted here in Romans 13:11–14 and in Mark 13:13; Matthew 24:43; and Luke 12:39 and 21:28, 36. There are also possible allusions to the Jesus tradition concerning tribute money in Romans 13:1–7 (cf. Mark 12:13–17); concerning divorce in 1 Corinthians 7:10 (Mark 10:2–12; Matt. 5:32 and 19:9); on earning one's keep by living out the Gospel in 1 Corinthians 9:14 (cf. Gal. 6:6; 1 Tim. 5:17–18; Matt. 10:10; Luke 10:7); and on eating what is put in front of you in 1 Corinthians 10:27 (cf. Luke 10:8).

Some commentators have even found possible references to the Gospel tradition in 2 Corinthians 10:1 on the meekness and gentleness of Christ (cf. Matt. 11:29); on the humility and death of Christ in Philippians 2:6–11 (cf. Luke 22:27; John 13:4); and on Christ not pleasing himself (Mark 14:36). In all of this the question is: Are these simply fortuitous parallels or do they suggest Paul's knowledge of Jesus' own teaching? Some continuity is suggested here in the broadest sense, but we cannot claim on the basis of such parallels that Paul actually knew words of Jesus.

In view of these various considerations it can only be said that the picture of the relation between Jesus and Paul looks extremely foggy. The absence of any reference to major aspects of Jesus' life and teaching familiar to us from the synoptic Gospels seems very strange. For some commentators, Paul most likely preached the Gospel in places like Corinth and Thessalonica by using Jesus' parables and miracles and his message of the kingdom of God, and did not, therefore, need to include the material in his letters—which are in any case concerned with specific problems raised by specific communities. Paul's letters are also by nature discursive and do not lend themselves to lengthy narrative sections. The problem with this, however, is that it is an argument from silence; there is no evidence that Paul preached using Gospel material and so didn't need to tell his communities a second time. Another argument is based on 2 Corinthians 5:16, where Paul says that whereas he once regarded Christ "from a human point of view," he does so no more. Some commentators have interpreted this to mean that whereas Paul once approached Christ as a human being, he does so no more, meaning that since his Damascus experience Paul has seen Christ in relation to God and is not, therefore, interested in purely historical matters. However, this does not seem to be the real meaning of the verse. It probably refers to Paul's humanity: whereas he had once looked at Christ simply from the point of view of a human being, he now sees more in him after his life-changing experience. He is seeing Jesus, as it were, from a God's-eye point of view. In any case, it is clear that for Paul it is the *significance* of Jesus in relation to God and to human faith that Paul is interested in and not straightforward historical data in the narrower sense. Concerning the other matters discussed here, the "traditions" of which Paul speaks may well go back a long way. He knows of the meal that Jesus ate with his disciples the night before he died, of his death on a cross, and of details relating to his resurrection. These provide substantial links with the historical figure of Jesus even if details are lacking. As for the material in Paul which overlaps with that in the Gospels, the links are too tentative to build any serious view of a close connection between Jesus and Paul upon them. Only a possible line of continuity can be established.

Paul and Jesus on the Law

One way of approaching the question of the relation between Jesus and Paul is to try to establish their respective views on the Torah. This is a notoriously difficult task, but the attempt at least points up some of the methodological problems inherent in the whole process and can function as something of a test case. Both Paul and Jesus were born into the Judaism of their day and both obviously had attitudes toward the Torah. However, difficulties arise immediately, and once again they are over the sources. There is the basic fact, as we have noted, that all the data we have on Jesus comes from a time after Paul. Because of this and because of conflicting material in the Gospels, it is very difficult to establish what Jesus' attitude to the law actually was. A similar problem of getting a clear picture also arises in the case of Paul because there is so much material from different contexts in his ministry. However, although there has been a great deal of disagreement about the matter, it is possible to see coherence in Paul's material concerning the law.

It is well known that Paul himself was "born under the law" (Gal. 4:4) and grew up under the law. The law was the backbone of Paul's life from childhood in Tarsus through to his dramatic

Damascus experience of Jesus. Indeed, Paul himself claims that he was "under the law blameless" (Phil. 3:6), which reflects just how seriously he must have kept it. For Paul, the law was God's way of communicating with humankind; it had been given by Moses at Sinai; was the seal of the covenant; and had even been "ordained by angels" (Gal. 3:19). However, after his dramatic Damascus experience, Paul's perception of God, and of his dealings with Israel and humankind generally, changed. He now saw that in Jesus Christ God had done something radically new, something that overtook what Paul had so far believed about the law and Israel. Now, God was offering new paths for inclusion of the Gentiles into his purposes. Now "in Christ," the law no longer had the central place it had had. But God had not changed his mind. His plans were being worked out gradually across history.

In his letters to the Romans and the Galatians, Paul writes to two very different communities concerning the law. Because of this he makes a number of seemingly contradictory statements, but his basic line is that the law is God's gift to his people and is therefore "holy" (Rom. 7:12). Jesus Christ is the "end of the law" (Rom. 10:4) but in the sense of fulfillment rather than final end. In some ways, it is in Galatians that the clearest picture of Paul's attitude to the law can be seen. Using the illustration of the *paidagogos* (school teacher or nanny), Paul claims that the law was necessary until Christ came (Gal. 3:24). The nanny is necessary until such time as the child has grown up. He or she then no longer needs the nanny, although the nanny has been indispensable for a period. So with the law, it was given by God and was indispensable to Israel until Christ came. But now "in Christ" it is no longer necessary. In this way Paul is able to show how the law is both necessary and yet fulfilled and overtaken in Christ.

With this broad picture of Paul's attitude to the law in mind, we can now turn to Jesus. We have already drawn attention to the difficulties of establishing Jesus' views from material that comes from a later time. There are certainly different views of the Jewish law in the Gospels, and it is hard to find a single view that belonged to Jesus. However, the evangelists do present Jesus in relation to the law. Limiting our investigation to the first three Gospels, we can see from Mark and the parallels in Matthew and Luke that Jesus occasionally challenges the law. For example, he challenges the Sabbath law when his disciples walk through the cornfields on the Sabbath plucking heads of corn (Mark 2:23–28 *et par.*) and when he heals someone on the Sabbath (Mark 3:1–6 *et par.*). It is in Matthew's Gospel, however, that perhaps the clearest attitude to the law among the synoptic writers can be found. Here, Jesus' view is that the law and everything to do with it will remain in place until the end of time (Matt. 5:17f.). The "antitheses" in Matthew's Sermon on the Mount ("You have heard it said . . . but I say to you," Matt. 5:21–48) seem to show Jesus contradicting the law, but it is clear that here and elsewhere Jesus is radicalizing the law rather than challenging it.

The basic problem or question with these passages is whether we are dealing here with the views of Jesus or those of the evangelists. What we can say is that there is a distinct difference of emphasis between Matthew on the one hand and Mark and Luke on the other (see Matt. 22:34–40; cf. Mark 12:28–34 and Luke 10:25–37). Overall, it seems that Jesus was probably a radicalizer of the law, one who saw its continuing significance but also the need to see it in perspective. The perspective in Matthew does seem to belong more to Matthew than to Jesus. The final problem here is this: if Jesus had a clear teaching on the Jewish law or attitude toward the law, then presumably this would have been known to his followers and perhaps to his persecutors. In this case, why would Paul need to work through his attitude to the law so much in his letters, showing no sign of any awareness of any teaching of Jesus on the subject?

Our investigation has shown that the material on the law in Paul is complex, although there is coherence in what he has to say. The law is fully part of God's purposes and yet it has been fulfilled and brought to its fullness in Christ. Although there is an ambiguity in what Paul says, it is also true that he was writing to different circumstances with different needs. When it comes to the Gospels, it is clear that there are major problems attributing to Jesus what may come from the evangelists, and Matthew especially seems to reflect his own attitude to the law in his portrayal of Jesus. However, if anything can be gleaned on this subject from the Gospels, it is that Jesus was not against the law, as has sometimes been claimed. He was rather a radicalizer of the law, one who wanted to reinterpret the law in the context of his own ministry. The complexity of all this means that it is a bold commentator indeed who would wish to make a final judgment on the relation between Jesus and Paul on the law. We can only conclude that while Jesus radicalizes the law in the context of Judaism, especially in Mark's Gospel, Paul reinterprets it as the "apostle to the Gentiles."

Paul and Jesus in Acts

Finally, we turn to the question, "What does the Paul of Acts know about Jesus?" In many ways we are at a double disadvantage with this question, as Acts was written by Luke, and both Paul and Paul's view of Jesus in Acts are part of Luke's theology. They are, therefore, part of the Lukan presentation. However, there is no reason to be completely skeptical about the historical reliability of Acts, and it is certainly worth noting what material there is.

Within the context of Luke's wider theology in Luke-Acts and in the context of his presentation of Paul as "apostle to the Gentiles," certain things appear concerning Jesus. In fact, most of the material appears in speeches made by Paul. As in Paul's letters, there is a noticeable lack of any narrative account of the events of Jesus' life such as we find in the Gospels, although there are outlines in the speeches down to chapter 13. Once again there are no birth stories, parables, miracles, or accounts of Jesus' death and resurrection. The interest is more in the significance, meaning, and interpretation of Jesus as Lord than in historical detail. As in Paul's letters, key elements are present. The resurrection of Jesus is central

(13:29f., 36; 17:31), and Paul obviously knows of Jesus' death (13:29). He sees Jesus as Son of God (9:20); as Christ (18:5); and as "Lord" (9:5; 20:19, 21, 24, 28; 21:13; 22:8, 10, 19; 26:15); as someone who preached the kingdom of God (19:8; 20:25; 28:23, 30–31); and whose purpose and significance were to be seen in relation to David and the prophets (13:16–52; 28:23). Also, John the Baptist pointed forward to Jesus (13:24); and Pilate had him killed even though he was innocent (13:28).

Perhaps the most interesting and significant verse in terms of a search for a link with the historical Jesus himself is Paul's apparent quotation of Jesus in his speech in Miletus ". . . remembering the words of the Lord Jesus 'It is more blessed to give than to receive'" (20:35). In fact, these words of Jesus are nowhere to be found in any of the Gospels. They are probably better seen as part of Luke's theology of wealth and poverty. In all, not a lot is gained through looking at Paul and Jesus in Acts, although it is significant that Luke's Paul has some parallels with the Paul of the letters: what Paul knows about Jesus is that he died, was buried, was raised and appeared, and that he is Christ, Son of God, and Lord.

What, then, can we conclude about the relation between Paul of Tarsus and Jesus of Nazareth? Contrary to the views of some scholars it cannot be said with any certainty that the two men ever met. Paul was probably born around the same time as Jesus and he certainly knew of Jesus and his teaching; he was, after all, a persecutor of the followers of Jesus. But all this does not mean that we know that he met Jesus. As to how much Paul knew of the tradition that surrounded Jesus, we have seen enough to be confident of a connection, but beyond noting parallel points, detail is lacking. It is certainly true that Paul is mostly interested in the significance of the events he recounts, rather than their historical factuality. Paul is certainly not as interested in the "historical Jesus" as many would like him to be. In any case the distinction between the "Jesus of history" and the "Christ of faith" is itself modern. Even so, we must face the possibility that Paul may not have known major features of the "life of Jesus" as it is popularly imagined today. Paul may not have known of Jesus' birth in Bethlehem or his parables and miracles.

But Paul does have strong connections with what he calls "tradition," and there is no need to be skeptical that Paul's traditions relating to the Last Supper and to Jesus' death and resurrection constitute strong connections with the Jerusalem church and maybe even with Jesus himself. Where sayings of Jesus appear to have overlaps or parallels in Paul's letters we have seen that verbal connections and even similar attitudes to subjects do not mean that Paul knew the Jesus tradition. In a major test case, that of Jesus' and Paul's attitudes to the Jewish law, we have seen that major methodological problems come to the fore. The attitudes of both Jesus and Paul to the law have been variously interpreted, and although we have great detail from Paul's letters, there is a significant problem in establishing Jesus' attitude. Not much can be gleaned on the basic subject from the Acts of the Apostles. Given this situation, it is clear that the question of the relation between Jesus and Paul is locked in a certain circularity and is likely to remain a conundrum.

THREE

PAUL AND EPHESUS
TEXTS, HISTORY, AND
ARCHAEOLOGY

The mention of Ephesus in the context of a conversation about St. Paul usually brings to mind the epistle to the Ephesians and Paul's encounter with Demetrius and the silversmiths in Acts 19. Beyond these, many people would be hard put to think of any connection between Paul and Ephesus. It is widely known, of course, that Ephesus is important in early Christianity generally: there is the tradition of the apostle John and Mary the mother of Jesus living there after Jesus' death, and of John's Gospel being written there. There is also the great council of Ephesus of 431 which marks a major turning point in the development of early Christianity. However, these are all after the time of Paul and shed no light whatever upon his involvement with Ephesus.

The widespread ignorance of the significance of Ephesus for Paul is unfortunate, for the city probably had considerable bearing on his life and letters and on the subsequent development of his theology. For example, a number of Paul's letters were probably written from Ephesus; it is possible that he was imprisoned there; and it was highly likely the center of the development of Pauline Christianity after the apostle's death. In spite of all this, Ephesus has been overshadowed in the popular imagination by the places to which Paul certainly wrote letters, for example Corinth, Galatia, and Rome.

The aim of this chapter is to draw attention to the importance of Ephesus for Paul and for the development of Pauline Christianity after his death, and also to illustrate something of what the city was really like when Paul was there. In order to do this, I shall: first, outline the probable extent of Paul's involvement with Ephesus; second, note the importance of Ephesus as a center of Pauline Christianity into the second century; and third, consider briefly the history of Ephesus and the archaeological excavations there to see what light these shed on the city in Paul's day.

Paul in Ephesus

What exactly was the extent of Paul's involvement with Ephesus? How long was he there, and how do we know? First of all, to approach this question through the epistle to the Ephesians and Acts 19 is very misleading. Many commentators are now of the opinion that Paul did not write Ephesians, and Acts 19 comes from the pen of Luke later in the first century and is therefore, strictly speaking, a secondary source for matters concerning Paul. This does not mean that Ephesians and Acts are not important texts in the wider quest for Paul's relation to Ephesus. Indeed, as we shall see, Ephesians plays a crucial role in tracking how Pauline Christianity developed in and around Ephesus after Paul's death, and Acts provides important material in relation to the chronology of Paul's ministry. However, it makes more sense to turn first to the letters that Paul himself wrote in order to see where Ephesus features in his life and ministry.

Let us begin with a simple observation: when we think of the important cities of Paul's ministry, we usually name the places to which his letters were sent. Counting the letters that Paul undoubtedly wrote, that would mean Corinth, Thessalonica, Philippi, Rome, and Galatia. These, of course, are important places in Paul's life, and reading his letters in the light of history and archaeological excavations gives us a vivid sense of his life and ministry in those places. However, it is equally important from the point of view of understanding Paul to ask where he himself was when he wrote his letters. His own context at the time of writing is just as important as that of those to whom he was writing. Modern readers turning to Paul's letters usually remain completely ignorant of Paul's own context of writing. In many cases, of course, we may not know for certain where Paul was when he wrote a letter and a good deal of hypothesizing becomes necessary. Yet if we follow this approach, it rapidly becomes clear that Ephesus featured much more in Paul's life and ministry than Ephesians and Acts alone might indicate.

The first mention of Ephesus in Paul's own letters can be found in 1 Corinthians. At the end of that letter Paul indicates that he is in Ephesus at the time of writing (1 Cor. 16:8). First Corinthians is usually thought to have been written in the early 50s of the first century, so Paul would have been in Ephesus then. It is widely known that 1 Corinthians was not an entirely "successful" letter and that Paul had to write to the Corinthians again. Many commentators are of the view that some parts of 2 Corinthians, which is almost certainly a collection of a number of different letters, might also have been written from Ephesus. Furthermore, the letter to the Galatians might have been written around the same time as 1 Corinthians and could also have come from Ephesus, although the letter itself does not indicate this. It has also been suggested that some of the other letters that bear Paul's name were written from Ephesus, especially the so-called "letters from prison" or "captivity epistles," that is, Philippians, Colossians, Ephesians, and Philemon.

Any consideration of Paul's letters from prison raises questions of where and when he was imprisoned and of how many imprisonments there were (cf. 2 Cor. 11:23). A number of locations have been suggested for Paul's imprisonments. In Acts, Philippi (16:23), Caesarea (23:23–26:32), and Rome (28:16) are mentioned. Early traditions outside the New Testament tell of Paul's final days in

Rome (Eusebius, *Church History* 2.22.2), but there is also an early tradition of his imprisonment in Ephesus (*Acts of Paul* 7). Paul himself refers to having "fought with beasts in Ephesus" (1 Cor. 15:32), which some have thought to be a reference to an imprisonment there. In spite of real difficulties in establishing the location of Paul's imprisonments, many commentators are now confident that an imprisonment in Ephesus is highly likely. If Paul was imprisoned in Ephesus, then, depending on the dating of the various letters involved, it is at least possible that the letters from prison were written from there.

Answers to all these questions are bound up in the complexity of determining the overall chronology of Paul's life and ministry. But if a Pauline imprisonment in Ephesus is taken seriously, and if the letters from prison were written from Ephesus, then it looks as though most of the authentically Pauline letters might have been written from there apart from Romans and 1 Thessalonians; and some have even claimed that Romans 16, a chapter consisting largely of greetings to a number of individuals, was originally written to the Christians in Ephesus. The presence of Prisca and Aquila, who had probably gone from Corinth to Ephesus, has, among other things, given rise to this idea (cf. Rom. 16:3). In view of all this, no wonder an early Christian tradition claims that Paul founded the church in Ephesus (Irenaeus, *Against Heresies* 3.3.4).

One must, of course, be careful in the absence of hard evidence not to get carried away with the idea that Paul wrote most of his letters from Ephesus. But the overall thrust of the evidence we have suggests that Ephesus was at least far more significant in Paul's life and ministry than is popularly imagined.

Ephesus after Paul

Ephesus was not only important as a base or "headquarters" for Paul and his letter-writing; it was also important in the development of his theology and in the editing and collecting of his letters after his death. There are New Testament texts that are important in relation to this: the epistle to the Ephesians and Acts 19 can now be investigated; there are "deutero-Pauline" letters, namely the Pastoral Epistles, which mention Ephesus; and a theory involving Philemon, Colossians, and Ephesians maintains that Paul's letters were collected in and around Ephesus. All of this indicates that Ephesus was indeed *a* center if not *the* center of Pauline Christianity as it developed into the second century.

Let us turn first to the epistle to the Ephesians. Why can this letter not be taken seriously as a primary source for information about Paul and Ephesus? The first thing is that many commentators now think that Paul himself did not write this letter. In the ancient world people frequently wrote under a pseudonym, perhaps the name of their leader, in order to give their letter more authority. This was a common practice and in no way reflected badly on the author using the pseudonym. In the case of Paul, his followers wrote in his name after his death as his theology needed interpretation in different situations and in a different era of Christian life. A crucial question here, of course, is "Why do people think Paul himself is not the author of this letter?" The argument for "pseudonymity" where the so-called deutero-Pauline letters are concerned is usually based on matters of style, vocabulary, and content, and in many cases a letter reflects a different ethos from that of the authentically Pauline letters. Although commentators are divided over the authenticity of Ephesians it is widely thought to be post-Pauline on the above grounds and cannot, therefore, be used to tell us directly about Paul's own association with Ephesus.

Second, and more serious than this, the epistle to the Ephesians was probably not written specifically to the Christians in Ephesus in any case. The words in the opening address, "Paul, an apostle of Christ Jesus by the will of God, to the saints who are at Ephesus" (1:1), contain a textual variant, that is, words that are not in all the early manuscripts of the letter. The words that are absent in the earliest manuscripts are *who are at Ephesus (en Epheso)*. The implication of this is that the letter was not aimed specifically at Ephesus but was perhaps a circular letter written to a number of different churches in the Ephesus area, of which Ephesus was one. In any case, Ephesians is singularly uninformative about its addressees wherever they were. For these reasons, we must be very careful in making any specific claims about Paul and Ephesus from the text of Ephesians itself.

If we are now thinking of texts that were written after the time of Paul we can turn to Acts 19. Acts indicates that Paul was in Ephesus on two occasions: once, briefly on the second missionary journey (18:19–21), and again for a longer period of two years on the third missionary journey (19:1–41). Paul seems to have spent between two and three years in Ephesus early on in his ministry, although in Acts 20:31 he specifically says it was three years. Acts 19 is the chapter specifically concerned with Paul in Ephesus and consists of a number of distinct sections: (a) material relating to the Holy Spirit and to the baptism of John (vv. 1–7); (b) speaking in the synagogue and the Hall of Tyrannus (vv. 8–10); (c) miracles performed through Paul's handkerchiefs and aprons (vv. 11–20); (d) travel plans (vv. 21–22); and (e) the incident with Demetrius and the silversmiths (vv. 23–41). All of these take place in Ephesus. The main problem with this material, however, as we have already noted, is that it comes from a period much later than that of Paul and reflects the theological scheme and concerns of Luke. The material on Paul and the Jews, and on Paul and the cult of Artemis, for example, seems to reflect relations in Ephesus in Luke's day rather than in Paul's. At the very least, however, Ephesus is a key location for Paul in Luke's portrayal of the development of Christianity in Acts.

The next thing to note is the presence of Ephesus in other deutero-Pauline letters. The references are all in the first two of the so-called Pastoral Epistles, 1 and 2 Timothy. These letters are almost unanimously thought not to be by Paul. They are pseudonymous writings from a later hand and reflect a distinctively different and developed ecclesiastical situation and ethos from anything Paul might have known. They are the work of an author writing under Paul's name a generation later and pointing Timothy in the direction of sound doctrine and practice. Insofar as Ephesus itself is concerned, the Pastorals show that Timothy is in Ephesus (1 Tim. 1:3); Onesiphorus is in Ephesus (2 Tim. 1:16–18); and Tychicus has been sent to Ephesus (2 Tim. 4:12). In the light of these references and the general situation that the Pastorals reflect we can conclude that there was a Christian community in Ephesus probably in the early years of the second century. Indeed there is a later tradition found in Eusebius in the fourth century that Timothy had been Bishop of Ephesus (*Church History* 3.4.5.).

Questions concerning life and events in Ephesus in the years following Paul's death are difficult to answer with any certainty, but a theory originally put forward in 1935 by John Knox in his book *Philemon among the Letters of Paul* opens up an exciting string of possibilities that point once again to the importance of Ephesus in Pauline Christianity after Paul. Knox's work is primarily a study of Paul's letter to Philemon, but it spans out into a much wider hypothesis concerning the relation of Philemon to Colossians, to Ephesians, and to the collection of Paul's letters in the generation after him. The theory is very convincing. Knox claims that Onesimus, the slave on whose behalf Paul wrote his letter to Philemon (who probably resided in Colossae), later became bishop of Ephesus in the second century. Ignatius's letter to the Ephesians, written in the early second century, mentions an Onesimus as Bishop of Ephesus, and there are significant literary parallels between Ignatius's letter and Philemon. Knox emphasizes the personal nature of Paul's letter to Philemon: he is writing on behalf of the slave Onesimus because he himself wants Onesimus to be free for service in the Gospel. Actually, Knox thinks that Archippus (to whom the letter is co-addressed) is the real owner of Onesimus and that Philemon is in charge of the churches in the wider area. Ephesus, Colossae, and Laodicea were all cities within the same area of the Lycus Valley in western Asia Minor. Knox goes on to show that the letter to Philemon is closely connected to the epistle to the Colossians. The letter refers to an overlap of characters, including Onesimus (Col. 4:7–9), and of subject, namely slaves

(Col. 3:22–4.1). Knox also notes the well-known dependence of Ephesians on Colossians. The Ephesian passage on slaves has different emphases (Eph. 6:5–9), but there is significant dependence on Colossians. From these close literary and geographical connections Knox infers that Onesimus the slave collected Paul's letters together. Knox suggests that in doing so, Onesimus depended considerably on Colossians as he himself wrote Ephesians as a letter that bound the whole collection together. He also included Paul's letter to Philemon because of his own personal involvement with it originally. This process of collecting, editing, and interpreting Paul's letters and theology took place in Ephesus where Onesimus was bishop. Even if the finer detail of Knox's theory cannot be substantiated, he has nevertheless given us here an incredible insight into the way in which Paul's letters might have been gathered together after his death, and it is significant that Knox thinks that Ephesus was at the center of this process.

In surveying material from the period immediately following Paul, then, it certainly seems that Ephesus was a center of gravity. From Acts, the Pastoral Epistles, and Knox's theory, it turns out to be a key city for Pauline Christianity; and the epistle to the Ephesians may have played a crucial role after all.

Ephesus: History and Archaeology

If the city of Ephesus was so important to Paul and the development of his theology, what sort of a place was it in his day and why might he have chosen it as a base? The history of Ephesus is long and fascinating, and though it is impossible to do full justice to the city in a short space, it is certainly worth noting some features of the city's history and making some observations gleaned from the archaeological excavations there. Ephesus was one of the most significant cities of the ancient world, especially for early Christianity. By Paul's time it was an old city, having been founded sometime c. 1000 BCE. In the sixth century BCE it already focused on the famous Temple of Artemis; in the fourth century BCE it was Hellenized under Alexander the Great and his successors; and in the second century BCE it was taken by the Romans and made the capital of the Roman province of Asia. Ephesus stood on the west coast of Anatolia (modern Turkey) on the Aegean Sea, on a natural harbor into which the Caister River flowed from an inland area of hills and valleys. The significance of the city lay in its port, which formed its contact with other major cities of the Mediterranean. Because of its port it was a major center of trade and commerce, and of the transmission of music, art, philosophy, culture, and learning. By Paul's time, Ephesus had already produced the poet Hipponax (c. 540 BCE); the philosopher Heraclitus (died after 480 BCE); and the painter Parrhasius (fifth/fourth century BCE) among others. The material remains that have been uncovered at the site in the last century or so indicate a wealthy, multicultural, cosmopolitan city, a metropolis whose significance in the Mediterranean world was considerable and whose influence spread well beyond the confines of Asia Minor.

On a visit to Ephesus today, the traveler will see one of the most impressive archaeological sites in the world, second only perhaps to Pompeii. The site was excavated in the nineteenth and early twentieth centuries by John Wood and David Hogarth on behalf of the British Museum. The impressive excavations and reconstructions seen in Ephesus today aid the imagination on its journey back to the ancient world, and one can see quickly why the city was so important. The "golden age" of Ephesus, however, came after Paul in the fourth and fifth centuries, and today's visitor must be careful not simply to slot Paul into the reconstructed site. Much of what is seen in Ephesus today would not have existed at the time of Paul, and some structures which Paul would have known have been destroyed. Among the many structures that have been uncovered or reconstructed are: the odeion; the state agora; the baths; the public toilets; the so-called slope or flank houses; several temples to gods and to emperors; the library of Celsus; the commercial agora; the famous theater; the once-colonnaded street down to the sea; the church of Mary, the probable scene of the

Council of Ephesus in 431; and some remains of a stadium. The archaeological discoveries at Ephesus indicate a multicultural metropolis, and even though many of these structures date from the second century onwards, first-century Ephesus was similarly a flourishing cosmopolitan city with religious, political, and economic links throughout the wider world.

Among the structures that were certainly standing in Paul's day were the stadium, which has of course been linked to Paul's having "fought with beasts" (1 Cor. 15:32), and the theater, which was being developed during Paul's time (cf. Acts 19:28f.). Yet interestingly, by far the most significant structure of the Ephesus of Paul's day was the temple of Artemis, of which there are no contemporary remains other than a single reconstructed pillar on a site between the main archaeological site and the area dominated by the remains of the Byzantine Basilica of St. John the Divine. The Temple of Artemis had a long and complex history stretching over a thousand years and incorporating several different stages of development. The final stage was that of the temple that Paul would have known. That temple was destroyed in c. 262 CE. Artemis was arguably the most popular goddess of the ancient Greek world. She was primarily a nature goddess, and was associated with Cybele of the Anatolians and Diana of the Romans. Her cult spread far and wide and great ritual was attached to her worship. Many of the gods and goddesses of ancient Greece and Rome were represented in Ephesus, but Artemis was the most significant; the temple dedicated to her ranked as one of the Seven Wonders of the ancient world. Even if Acts 19 is a text from a later period and tells us more about the church in Ephesus in Luke's day than in Paul's, Luke's setting is thoroughly realistic, although no remains have been found either of the synagogue or of the Hall of Tyrannus (Acts 19:8, 9).

It is clear from all this that in Paul's day Ephesus would have been considerably less grand than it later became. The archaeological site at Ephesus today speaks more of the Ephesus of later centuries than of Paul's day, but even then it was already an ancient and well-established city; it had a port that connected it with the rest of the Mediterranean world; it was cosmopolitan, with a rich mix of cultures and traditions; and it was a crossroads of religions and philosophies. In view of all this, Ephesus understandably played a key role in the rapid urbanization of Christianity from an early time. For Paul, Ephesus was not just a convenient headquarters; it was a powerful organ in his central task of taking the Gospel out into the many different cultures of the Roman world.

For anyone who imagined that the significance of Ephesus in Paul's life and letters could be established through looking at Ephesians and Acts alone, and that it didn't really matter very much anyway, the picture should now have changed! A brief look at some of Paul's letters and some theories concerning their date and place of writing indicates that Ephesus was perhaps the most significant city of Paul's ministry. Quite a few of his letters were probably written from there, and it seems highly likely that the city played a key role in the whole process of editing and collecting his letters a generation after his death. The deutero-Pauline references to Ephesus certainly give the impression that there was a Christian community there in the late first century and that the city had its own bishop in the early second century. In terms of the history and archaeology of the city, it is immediately clear that Ephesus was a major, capital city of Asia Minor. Its position on the Aegean Sea with its port made it a gateway through which much of the known world might pass. With the Temple and cult of Artemis, and with a rich melting pot of culture, religion, and philosophy around him, Paul used the city as his base for travel and preaching. In many ways Ephesus typifies the diversity of cultural contexts into which Paul took the Gospel, and it played a key role in equipping him for his task. In the light of all that has been gleaned here from New Testament texts, history, and archaeology, and even though there may be disagreement over specific arguments, there seems little doubt that Ephesus was a very significant city both for Paul himself and for later Paulinism.

FOUR

CONTEXTUALIZING PAUL
MARRIAGE AND SLAVERY IN 1 CORINTHIANS

S t. Paul the apostle has been portrayed in so many different ways over the centuries that it sometimes feels quite impossible to get a grip on what his attitudes to particular issues really were. In matters such as sex and marriage, community living, Christian worship, the role of women, and the place of slaves in society, Paul's attitude has mostly been portrayed as totally negative. But is such a view of Paul fair and does it do justice to the letters he actually wrote and the contexts in which he actually worked?

Although there has been a great deal of research over the last century into the world in which Paul lived, his letters are still often read out of context and through the lenses of later concerns. At the popular level, the subtleties of Paul's struggle with particular problems and the real gist of what he has to say are still not appreciated. If ancient Corinth was riddled with sexual promiscuity, is there any wonder that Paul might be cautious about sex? If Christian slaves in Corinth were indeed quite well off, is it surprising that Paul might have told them to stay in their present roles as slaves? The issues, of course, are complex and multifaceted, but it is at least clear that Paul has frequently been misrepresented through ignorance of his real historical context.

In this chapter, I first provide an overview of the historical, philosophical, and theological climate in ancient Corinth at the time of Paul; and second, I examine Paul's attitude in his first letter to the Corinthians to two major constellations of issues that confronted him: (a) marriage, divorce, and sexual relations; and (b) slavery.

Ancient Corinth at the Time of Paul:
Historical, Philosophical, and Theological Issues

What was Corinth actually like when Paul wrote his letters to the Christians there in the 50s of the first century CE? There are three important areas to consider: first, the historical, geographical, and cultural aspects of ancient Corinth. Here we shall look at the location and history of Corinth and how these affected the way people lived; second, the philosophical and moral outlook that shaped the lives and actions of the Corinthians. Here our concern will be with Corinthian gnosticism and the philosophical separation of spirit and body; and third, eschatology, or the belief that God would act radically and soon to bring about the end of the world. These three areas all played a significant part in Corinthian life and bore on Paul's reactions to the problems that confronted him in the community. Let us consider them in turn.

First, the historical, geographical, and cultural aspects of ancient Corinth. Ancient Corinth was a vibrant city that stood on the ridge of land connecting mainland Greece to the Peloponnese. It was a land route as well as a sea route, and like many of the cities to which Paul wrote letters, it was significant geographically, historically, economically, socially, and culturally. Many visitors passed through by land and sea; the city was multiethnic and multicultural; and it was a melting-pot of popular beliefs, religions, and philosophies. There had been an ancient city of Corinth long before Paul visited the area, but it had been destroyed by the Romans in 146 BCE. It was refounded by Julius Caesar in 46 BCE and had grown up like its predecessor to be socially diverse and culturally multilayered. Corinth was a wealthy city that hosted the famous Isthmian games on more than one occasion and was known probably above all for its work in bronze. By the time of Paul it had long been known, fairly or unfairly, as a place of indulgence and excess; even its name seems to come from a Greek word (*korinthiadsesthai*) whose root meaning is "to practice fornication." It was also famous for its Temple of Aphrodite with its reputed hundred thousand prostitutes. Little wonder that Paul had something to say about sexual relations. It is clear from 1 Corinthians that the young Christian community in the city had difficulties finding and establishing its identity. It was Paul's challenge to respond to their problems as constructively as he could in a culture that offered so many conflicting beliefs and lifestyles.

Second, the philosophical and moral outlook that shaped the lives and actions of the Corinthians. It seems that there were those in Corinth who assumed that they had a superior knowledge or *gnosis*. This *gnostic* tendency in Corinth was part of a religious trend that later fed into the Gnostic groups that flourished from the second century onwards. In the first century, however, it was more of a philosophical and religious tendency than a movement. The defining characteristic of this outlook was a dualism that separated mind and body, or spirit and matter. People overemphasized the importance of the spirit at the expense of the body. This emphasis on the spiritual in religious matters was one of the main problems Paul faced, for example in regard to belief about the resurrection. In terms of morals and daily living this worldview usually swung in one of two directions: either (1) indulgence of the body in food, drink, and sexual promiscuity (understandably, perhaps, in a city dominated by the temple of Aphrodite and its prostitution); or (2) total asceticism: the body simply didn't matter. In each case, exactly the same philosophical outlook led to a diametrically opposed lifestyle! These attitudes to life and the human body form an important part of the background to what Paul has to say about sexual relations.

Third, eschatology or the belief that the end of the world was imminent. During the period of the Second Jerusalem Temple (c. 536 BCE–CE 70) there were many strands of belief in Judaism about the coming end of the world. Each strand emphasized different elements in a broad spectrum of belief. All that need be noted here is the basic picture. Jews had always believed in a fundamentally active God, a creator who had called the people of Israel to himself and acted in bringing them out of Egypt and establishing the Covenant with them at Sinai. In line with this they believed that the same God would act for his people at the end of time. After the exile of 586 BCE, a prominent Jewish belief was that God would bring all Jews to Zion at the end of time and that they would in turn bring non-Jews with them. The literature of Judaism in the centuries preceding Jesus is peppered with a strong eschatological belief in God's final action for his people. In the years leading up to the destruction of the Second Temple and the fall of Jerusalem in CE 70, many Jews believed that this final action of God was very close. For some the emphasis was predominantly political, for others the emphasis was religious; but the overall belief was that time was short and that God would act very soon.

In the same period, the early Christians took over this Jewish eschatological worldview and recast it in terms of Jesus. For them it was God's action in Jesus that would finally bring in the end of time: he would return in a "second coming" or *Parousia* to bring about God's final purposes for his people. There were, of course, different emphases in the broad spectrum of Christian eschatological belief, but the focus was on the imminent return of Jesus and the imminent end of time. When Paul writes to the Corinthians he makes it clear that "the appointed time has grown very short" (1 Cor. 7:29), and that "the form of this world is passing away" (7:31).

These three groups of elements: the historical, geographical, and cultural; the philosophical and moral; and the eschatological, all bear on how Paul dealt with the problems that confronted him in Corinth. The Corinthian Christians lived in a multicultural society in which sexual promiscuity and physical indulgence as well as asceticism were rife. They also believed that the end of the present age would dawn very soon and that Jesus would return. When the Corinthians wrote to Paul asking him what they should do about certain problems in their community, they were not simply asking Paul for his opinions about matters of theoretical interest. They were faced with real cases and practical problems. As Paul responded, he struggled to enable them to discern how they should live in the short time left to them. What, then, did he have to say about marriage, divorce, sexual relations, and slavery?

Marriage, Divorce, and Sexual Ethics

Paul's teaching on marriage, divorce, and sexual relations can be found in 1 Corinthians 7. The first section of the chapter is verses 1–9. Marriage, divorce, and sexual relations are among those matters the Corinthians had already raised with Paul (v. 1). He now responds to their questions and concerns. We already know that there has been a case of sexual immorality in Corinth (5:1) and that Paul has reacted by advising that the person be cast out of the community (5:2). Once again here in chapter 7, sexual issues arise. The statement in 7:1, "It is well for a man not to touch a woman," has usually been taken to be Paul's view, but it is also possible that he is quoting the view of ascetic Corinthian Christians. In any case, Paul now begins his process of reasoning. Marriage is acceptable in his view, although it does also seem to be a concession to lust. There should be equality between the partners in marriage, he says, and each is to give the other their conjugal rights. Sex within marriage is certainly acceptable but, as in Judaism under the Torah, there can be periods of abstention by agreement. Indeed, it seems that sexual relations can be taken up in order to stave off the temptation of Satan. Paul says that he really wishes that people could remain single as he does (vv. 7–9), but he also knows that there are different states before God.

The usual interpretation of Paul here has been that marriage and sex are a concession: it is better to be single and celibate than to marry. The context, however, could suggest a different view. If sexual promiscuity and asceticism are both rife in Corinth, then Paul may be steering a middle path between the two. On the one hand, he says that sex is not the main focus in marriage and it is sometimes better to refrain from sexual relations. On the other hand, there is nothing wrong with sex and marriage, and it is better to marry than to burn with lust. Furthermore, if 7:1 is really a statement from the ascetic Corinthians, it casts a more positive light on Paul's general attitude. To the ascetics' negative views of sex, he says "there's actually nothing wrong with it in itself"!

In verses 10–16, Paul turns to the issue of divorce. Divorce between Christians is out of the question, and Paul says that his teaching here comes from "the Lord" (v. 10). Whether this comes from any knowledge Paul may have had of the tradition of Jesus' teaching on the matter is unclear (cf. Mark 10:2–12; Matt. 5:31–32; 19:3–12; Luke 16:18; and see Deut. 24:1–4), but he probably means that it has been revealed directly to him from the living Lord. In any case he takes a different basic line from that found in Deuteronomy 24, where a man may write a bill of divorce against his wife on the grounds of indecency. In ancient Judaism a man might divorce his wife but not a woman her husband. For the Jesus of the synoptic Gospels divorce is also out of the question, although there is Matthew's "exception clause" on the grounds of unchastity (Matt. 19:9). For Paul, it is better that there be no divorce among believers (1 Cor. 7:10–11). If a partner dies, the other can remarry (7:39). In cases of mixed marriages, however, Paul's attitude is different. It is now Paul's own view and not the Lord's that he gives (v. 12). If mixed marriages are functioning well there is no need to worry; the unbelieving partner is even consecrated through the believing partner (v. 14). However, if an unbelieving partner wishes to separate, it is as well that he or she should go.

In verses 25–40, after a change of focus, Paul returns to the question of marriage. The argument is still that it is better for people to remain as they are (v. 26). Paul now states clearly in verses 28 and 37 that marriage isn't a sin (is he speaking once again to the Corinthian ascetics?). His argument against marriage is also practical: he wants Corinthian Christians to be free from "worldly troubles" and "anxieties" (vv. 28, 32) that will prevent them from doing the work of the Lord. Some of the roots of the ideal of celibacy that was to dominate parts of the Christian tradition later can be found in these verses.

Overall, a consideration of the context in Corinth at the time of Paul shows that his attitude to marriage, divorce, and sexual relations may not be as negative as is often thought. Given the prevalence of sexual promiscuity in Corinth, it is not surprising to find Paul steering a middle path between two excessive attitudes toward the body and sex. Paul's beliefs about the imminent coming of the end of the world, linked with his theology of "calling," also bear on his attitude here: the time is short and Christians should stay in the role they were in when they were called. They should concentrate on matters relating to the Lord. If the popular portrayal of Paul's views on marriage, divorce, and sex can appear in a modified light through a consideration of the context in which he wrote, how do his comments about slavery appear when considered in their context?

Slavery

In 1 Corinthians 7:17–24, Paul turns briefly away from the question of marriage, divorce, and sexual relations to a section concerned primarily with "calling." He later turns back to marriage in verses 25–40. Paul's interest in "calling" binds verses 17–24 into chapter 7, and chapter 7 into the whole epistle. From 1:1 onwards Paul has had an eye on his own and others' calling (cf. 1:26). His message here in chapter 7 seems to be "stay where you are in your calling from God, whatever it is." Paul's attention in verses 17–24 now turns to two specific issues: circumcision and slavery. Our concern here is with the second. Paul refers to slaves in 7:22 and 23, and his message to them has often been perceived as negative. It is often assumed that if Paul is telling slaves to stay as they are in their slavery then he must be encouraging slavery, which can only be bad. Unfortunately, Paul's words about slaves have often been read through the lens of the nineteenth-century slave trade. The images connected with the slave trade of that period are largely ones of hard labor, physical and personal abuse, and death. Coupled with the fight for the abolition of the slave trade in the nineteenth century and for the liberation of slaves of different sorts ever since, this has left western readers of the Bible with very negative images of slavery. Read in the light of the slave trade, how strange it is that Paul seems to be saying in 1 Corinthians 7:21, "Were you a slave when called? Never mind." But Paul's letter to the Corinthians was not written in the nineteenth century, and the situation regarding slaves in Paul's day was totally different. In Paul's day, a slave could sometimes be much better off than someone who was free.

In Paul's day, slaves were treated differently under Greek, Roman, and Jewish law. It is certainly true that slaves could be treated badly, but in Greece especially they could be quite privileged. In ancient Greece slaves did not belong to one social class or level of wealth. They could be found anywhere along the social spectrum. Basically, the social class and the wealth of a slave depended upon that of his master. In Greek society there were three main categories: (1) slaves; (2) freemen; and (3) those in between (freedmen). Those in between were slaves who had been partly freed or manumitted and had gained a certain amount of independence. The process of manumission itself is quite instructive here as it opens up for us what the position of particular slaves might be. The slave was essentially owned by his master. Of course, he might have landed in that position by any of a number of different routes, e.g., by being born into a slave family or by selling himself into slavery. Whichever it was, his position as a slave could provide him with more security than if he were a free person. For this reason, the process of manumission had to be handled carefully and the slave had to be careful that he did not move from slavery into a worse position. Slaves, therefore, could be owned by very wealthy owners who treated them well and under whose terms they were able to build up their own wealth. For many, it could certainly be better to be a slave than to be free.

However, it seems that most slaves did wish to buy themselves out of slavery in the end, simply in order to gain their independence. The process of manumission had several levels, and freedom could be bought gradually across many years, the slave gaining independence in legal matters step by step. The famous manumission inscriptions at Delphi in Greece, dating from between 200 BCE and 75 CE, are mostly in the form of sales contracts in which the god Apollo played a key part in effecting the slaves' freedom. A slave could be "bought out" of slavery by a third party. Some commentators have thought it possible that this process of manumission influenced Paul's notion of salvation in 1 Corinthians 7:23, especially as he uses the idea there of being "bought with a price." In general, a slave might be wealthy but might stage his manumission to suit his own purposes in ensuring that he had secure independence when he was free. Slaves could of course be treated badly, but many might be comfortable and well off, and slavery in Greece in this period should not be equated with hard labor and abuse.

It was this sort of social situation regarding slaves that Paul found in Corinth. What was a slave to do if he had become Christian and the end of the world was imminent? In 1 Corinthians 7:17–24 Paul refers to slaves specifically. They were undoubtedly in different social situations, but they had asked Paul for his guidance. In 7:21 Paul is still speaking about "calling" and how Christians should remain in the state in which they were when they were called. We then find one of the most difficult verses in the New Testament, not only because of the more recent slave trade imagery often imposed upon it but also because of the problems with the grammar and logic of the Greek text itself: "Were you a slave when called? Never mind. But if you can gain your freedom, avail yourself of the opportunity." This translation seems to say: "Don't worry if you are a slave. On the other hand, if you can get freedom, take it." In the light of the coming end of the world, this makes good sense: a Christian might want to use the limited time left as a free person devoted to the Lord.

But the Greek of this verse is not so straightforward. The difficulty centers on the words *mallon chresai*, translated above as "avail yourself of the opportunity." They can equally well mean "make use of your present condition." This translation would render the verse "were you a slave when called? Never mind. But if you can gain your freedom make use of your present condition (instead)." The two translations say opposite things, and the problem of which translation bears Paul's real intention is completely insoluble from the Greek text. It is worth noting, however, that Paul has the habit in this chapter of stating a norm and then making an exception (cf. 7:2, 9, 11, 15, 36, and 37), and he could be doing the same here at verse 21: "Remain a slave, but if freedom arises, take it." On the other hand, he seems to be encouraging Christians throughout the passage to stay as they are. The sense of verse 21 would then be, "Remain a slave, and even if the possibility of freedom arises, take the opportunity to make the most of your status as slave." This latter would be because of the imminent end of the world. Commentators who have opted to focus on Paul's grammar have usually opted to translate the words as meaning "take freedom," while those who have concentrated on the context and general argument have usually opted for "take slavery." If slaves were sometimes in comfortable positions in Greek society, a positive attitude to slavery on Paul's part is not so shocking after all.

What, then, do we learn from this consideration of the social context of slaves in Paul's day? The social status of slaves in ancient Greece and the difficulties in translating Paul's Greek suggest that we must be very careful in interpreting Paul as encouraging a

horrific institution. On the contrary, he appears in a more positive light yet again; his concern is the primacy of one's Christian
"calling" whoever one is.

What has this consideration of Paul's historical context taught us
about how he responded to some of the problems confronting
him? We have seen that the context into which he wrote was
complex and varied. Ancient Corinth was a multicultural city
lying along major land and sea routes. The famous temple of
Aphrodite dominated Corinth, and the city was famed throughout the ancient world for prostitution and sexual promiscuity. The
climate of gnostic dualism led Christians to devalue their bodies;
some indulged them, while others starved them in asceticism. The
slaves in the city probably belonged to different social strata, and
some of them might have been very well off. Above all, there was
a powerful belief that the end of the world was coming very soon
and that Jesus would return imminently. Paul's teaching on marriage, divorce, sexual relations, and slavery are all affected by these
factors. He was not advising the Corinthians on ethical matters
for a long-term future, and anything he said had relevance only
for the interim period until the Lord returned. Paul tells the
Corinthian Christians that they are above all called by God and
it is ultimately better to concentrate on the things of God than
the things of this world, especially in the light of the return of
Jesus. No one really needed to change their positions before God
in the light of the coming end of time, he was saying. If they
needed to, they could marry; contrary to what many Corinthian
Christians might have thought, there was nothing sinful about it,
although Paul does think it is better to stay single. Regarding
slaves, if Paul is telling them to stay as they are, there is nothing
inherently wrong with that. Some of them might have been quite
well off, and the later nineteenth-century image of the slave needs
to be removed from the picture here. In the end, a consideration
of Paul's context modifies the negative image he has so often been
given and allows him to speak more clearly for himself.

FIVE

DISCERNING
THE BODY

FOOD, CONSCIENCE,
AND THE EUCHARIST
IN 1 CORINTHIANS

Throughout 1 Corinthians, Paul is concerned with building up a tragically divided Christian community. Very
early on in the letter it emerges that various factions in
Corinth are causing serious rifts (1:12). Paul's overriding concern
is to "build up" the church in Corinth and enable the diverse
body of believers to realize its inherent unity in Christ. In 1
Corinthians 12:12–31, Paul uses the image of the "body of
Christ" precisely for this purpose. First Corinthians was probably
written by Paul from Ephesus in the early 50s of the first century
CE. Apparently he had stayed in Corinth for eighteen months and
then left (Acts 18:11). A number of specific problems had arisen
since he left and he now responds to these in the letter.

One of the most significant of the problems appears in
1 Corinthians 8 and 10: it is whether followers of Christ should
or should not eat food that had been used in sacrifice to pagan
gods. This problem had clearly become an occasion of division for
the Corinthian Christians, and the way forward for them was by

no means clear. Paul's response was that it was a matter of conscience; it concerned not only the individual but also one's neighbor. Indeed, conscience turns out to be a crucial element for Paul in deciding how to behave in relation to the problem of food and therefore in building up the community. Another problem the Corinthians had raised with Paul concerned the eucharist, which had become an occasion of chaos and division (ch. 11). Once again, Paul's response is rooted in his concern to build up the community: "For any one who eats and drinks without discerning the body eats and drinks judgment upon himself" (11:29).

In this chapter, I first investigate Paul's attitude to eating food sacrificed to idols; second, I discuss the meaning of conscience in Paul's thinking; and third, I review Paul's teaching on the eucharist.

Food Sacrificed to Idols

The question of whether new followers of Christ should eat food that had been used in sacrifice to gods in pagan temples was particularly difficult for the Corinthian Christians. Paul's response was rooted in the notion of conscience and neighborly love. For those concerned, the matter was essentially practical: Could those who had now begun to follow Christ eat food that was associated in some way with their previous faith system? In one way or another, the problem affected everybody. For Jews who had turned to follow Christ, the problem was whether or not they still had to worry about the Jewish food laws. For converts from other religions, the question was whether or not they could eat meat that had been sacrificed to the gods of Greece and Rome. In both cases, the line between the old faith structure and the new one was blurred. In many cases new believers in Christ had retained beliefs and practices from their previous lives. Eventually questions arose as to what relation the other gods had to the Christian God; whether participating in events associated with them mattered; and whether such gods even existed in the first place.

In 1 Corinthians 8:1, Paul turns specifically to the matter of food sacrificed to idols. As in other matters already dealt with in this letter, his point of entry is the Corinthians' own notion of knowledge. The presence of a certain *gnosis* among the Christians in Corinth has been widely acknowledged for some time. It affected everything from their mindset to their practical living. Those who claimed they had this special "knowledge" operated on a dualism that separated spirit from body and mind from matter. It usually led them in one of two basic directions: bodily indulgence, on the ground that the body didn't matter, or bodily asceticism on the same grounds. In any case, the Corinthians undermined the importance of the physical creation to the extent that Paul reminds them their bodies are temples of the spirit (6:19; cf. 3:16–17). Now in chapter 8, his line is that the Corinthians' *gnosis* does nothing but inflate their arrogance. It is, rather, love, he says, which is the important thing. Indeed, this theme will form a dramatic climax in chapter 13 with the great hymn to love. Paul's approach in 1 Corinthians 8 is that the important thing for Christians is not to "know" but to "be known" by God.

It is here that the question of the very existence of other gods, or idols as Paul calls them, arises. Paul's overall point is that the whole problem about eating food offered to other gods is meaningless because those gods do not exist in the first place (8:4; cf. 8:8). Paul was aware that not all the Christians of Corinth knew this. There were some who were "weak" and behaved as if such gods did exist. Furthermore, the question of the existence of other gods raised the question of the nature of the God the Christians themselves worshipped. Paul writes here of the fundamental belief in one God and of Jesus Christ as Lord, through whom everything exists. His basic approach is theological and christological.

The central section of the argument about food comes in 8:7–13. The key question is whether Paul would eat meat that had been used in a sacrificial rite in a local temple if he were faced with it. The question at stake in this chapter is that of eating meat in a pagan temple: If Corinthians who now followed Christ were at a meal in a pagan temple that included meat sacrificed to the god of that temple, was it acceptable for them to eat it? In spite of his firm belief that it really didn't matter one way or the other because such gods didn't exist, the short answer from Paul was "no, he wouldn't eat it"! The heart of the argument has to do with "conscience," notably the weak consciences of other people present at a meal. Basically Paul's line was that, even though it didn't matter whether one ate the meat or not, and a Christian was free to eat the meat, there may be other people for whom (wrongly in Paul's view) it did matter. In this case such people must be acknowledged and honored even though they were "weak." If another person saw Paul eating meat that had been used in sacrifice to a pagan god and that person believed such gods were a reality, they would be scandalized. If they further believed that this issue mattered in the eyes of the Christian God and thought that Paul was acknowledging the existence of the other gods through his eating, then it would be better if Paul did not eat the meat. This was a matter of extreme importance, for a person's weak conscience might be wounded and damaged if he saw Paul eating the meat. Moreover, says Paul, such a thing is a "sin against Christ" (v. 12).

After an excursion into the nature of his own authority in 1 Corinthians 9, Paul returns specifically to the problem of food in chapter 10. He refers to the supernatural food and drink of the desert, to idolatry, and to the eucharist (vv. 16–17), before finally getting back to the practicalities of food sacrificed to idols. There is a seemingly different view in verse 21, where Paul says that the Corinthians cannot take part at the table of the Lord as well as at that of demons. But the explanation comes later. In verses 23–33, the matter is specifically addressed again. This time the scenario is different. Meat sacrificed in a pagan temple could be sold in the local markets and bought by local people. So, if there is a dinner party in the house of an unbeliever and a Christian is invited and is confronted with meat that has been used in sacrifice to pagan gods, that person need not worry about eating anything on the grounds of conscience (that is, his own conscience). If someone points out that the meat has been used in sacrifice, however, and he is worried about it, then the conscience of that person must be respected and scandal must be avoided. In this case, as in the previous example, Paul's response is that "for conscience' sake . . . do not eat it" (vv. 28–29). Here again, conscience plays a central role along with the notion of building up the community, which has been a major concern throughout the letter. Paul contrasts what is "lawful" with what "builds up," and seeking the good of the neighbor rather than the self is crucial.

Again, Paul uses the same basic argument as in chapter 8: eat whatever you like. He quotes Psalm 24:1 to support his view that the whole creation belongs to God. There then follow two of the most difficult verses of the New Testament (vv. 29–30), in which Paul asks why his liberty should be determined by scruples. It often seems that Paul is suddenly changing his mind here, especially in verse 30. But the issue is that he keeps his eye on the liberty of eating or not eating. Respect for the neighbor, and for weak consciences, is a superior form of liberty than simply doing what one likes regardless of the company one is keeping. Verse 30 does seem to give the opposite impression, and there are questions about the coherence of the text there. But Paul's response is basically the same in chapters 8 and 10: eating food that has been part of idol sacrifice doesn't matter in itself, because the pagan gods don't exist and everything in creation belongs to God anyway. But weak people might be worried and damaged in conscience if they see someone they respect eating the meat, especially if they don't understand that it doesn't matter. Regard for one's neighbor, or "discerning the body," is paramount in all this, and for the sake of a neighbor's conscience it is better not to eat the meat. If "conscience" is so central for Paul in responding to this problem, what exactly did he mean by this word?

Conscience

The word "conscience" comes from the Latin *conscientia* and is etymologically the same as the Greek equivalent *suneidesis*, both of which mean "knowledge with" oneself or another. Conscience is derived from "consciousness" in the sense of "consciousness of being in the wrong." Conscience was not a developed idea in the ancient world and has been interpreted in widely different ways down the centuries since. The many conflicting theological and philosophical notions of conscience bear witness to the fact that there is no single thing to which the word refers beyond the general sense. There is no clearly formed idea of conscience in the Hebrew Bible, nor is there a single equivalent Hebrew word. Paul, of course, wrote in Greek, and *suneidesis* has a very wide range of meanings. The context in which the word is used in a given case also bears considerably upon what it means. The word *suneidesis* is not used in the Septuagint and there is no specific word for conscience in Qumran or in the Rabbis. In Second Temple Judaism, a dominant notion was that the human person is ultimately governed by God, although there are ideas of the private and the public person and of conflict within a person. In Job 27:6 where the word *sunoida* occurs, there is the sense that inner conflict is possible. In Wisdom 17:11 we find a similar idea: conscience condemns wickedness within a person. There is, then, the sense of an element within a person that can come into operation and provide guidance for action.

The background to "conscience" in Paul and in the New Testament generally, however, is the everyday use of the word in ancient Greece. From about the sixth century BCE onwards, *suneidesis* had a predominantly negative or bad connotation and was associated with pain and unhappiness. Primarily, it had to do with the nature or order of things in the universe; it was related to the gods who provided that order and was sometimes seen as a divine element within people. Conscience was not primarily a moral faculty but soon became so. Those who were at odds with the order in creation were at odds with the gods and thus experienced pain and unhappiness. Conscience here had the sense of pain arising out of actions in the past which brought about disorder in the human person. There is thus the sense of inner tension and of accusation, witness and punishment arising within a person. There is rarely any notion of a "good conscience" as we know it today, although the absence of a bad conscience might be seen to be a good thing. The use of the word *suneidesis*, then, is very broad in ancient Greece, but it has a predominantly negative meaning and concerns past actions that produced pain within a person. Conscience was indicated by the sensation of pain that arose after an action and in the light of it, rather than a guiding principle that arose before an action.

In the Greek New Testament *suneidesis* (or a word of the same family) occurs thirty-one times, most frequently in Paul (1 Cor. 4:4; 8:7; 8:10, 12; 10:25, 27, 28, 29; 2 Cor. 1:12; 4:2; 5:11; Rom. 2:15; 9:1; 13:5). It also occurs in the Pastoral Epistles (1 Tim. 1:5, 19; 3:9; 4:2; 2 Tim. 1:3; Titus 1:15); Acts (23:1; 24:16); Hebrews (9:9, 14; 10:2, 22; 13:18); 1 Peter (2:19; 3:16, 21); and John (8:9, in a textual variant). There has been a great deal of disagreement over just how the New Testament uses of this word fit into the general background, but on the whole the uses are in line with the general breadth of meaning in the Greek world with its emphasis on negativity and pain following past actions.

However, there is also clearly something of a development in the use of the word across the New Testament texts. As we have already seen in 1 Corinthians 8 and 10, Paul seems to imply that conscience is fundamentally to do with knowing and acting in relation to others. In Romans, conscience is something that "bears witness," and is related to a person's place in society. In 2 Corinthians we learn of a "good conscience" (1:12) and of other people's knowledge of a person's conscience (4:2; 5:11). In the references in Acts and 1 Peter, we learn of a "good conscience" and a "clear conscience," while the Pastoral epistles indicate a connection between love, faith, and conscience. The most developed sense of conscience in the New Testament is found in Hebrews, where it is integrated into the wider theological scheme and associated with worship and the relation of the worshipper to Christ. The message there is that Christ's death has purified conscience (9:14) and produced a "clear conscience" (13:18).

In all this, it can be seen that the meaning of the word *sunei-desis* in Paul would have to do with negativity and pain about past actions, but that by his time it had also broadened out in meaning to include relations with other people in society. In Paul's reaction to the problem about food in 1 Corinthians, conscience is something that might be painful, and one person's actions can affect another's state of being for good or ill. It certainly does not just involve the individual: it is once again a question of "discerning the body." It is of great concern to Paul, then, that a member of the community consider the consciences of others in deciding how to act in relation to food. If conscience is such a driving element in Paul's response to the problem of food sacrificed to idols, how is it related to what he has to say about the eucharist?

The Eucharist

Paul's teaching on the eucharist appears in 1 Corinthians 11:23–34. As we have already seen, the theme of eating and drinking has been central to the chapters leading up to this. We have discussed Paul's response to the problem of food sacrificed to idols in chapters 8 and 10, and there has already been reference to "the cup of blessing," "the bread which we break" (10:16) and "the table of the Lord and the table of demons" (10:21). The connection between food and the eucharist for Paul is clear. Although he does not specifically mention conscience in chapter 11 it is clear that once again, concern for community and neighbor is paramount. Just as the occasions of eating food offered to idols can be places of offense, so the eucharist can be a place of division. It can also be a place of judgment and condemnation before God. An overriding concern of the whole letter has been division in the community, and it is no less the case here. It seems that the eucharistic gathering had become an occasion of abuse and disorder among the Corinthians. Paul was now writing to them about their gathering in order to bring them into line with his own views and those of the tradition.

The material in 1 Corinthians 11:23–34 is probably the earliest material on the eucharist in the New Testament. Paul may have received it from the Jerusalem church, and it could date back to the early years after the crucifixion of Jesus. Paul's approach in verse 23 is to relate what he has received from the tradition. In fairly technical language he speaks of *paradosis*, "handing over" or "handing on," in relation to what he has to say. The teaching is not from Paul himself; it comes from the experience, eucharists, and traditions of the earliest Christians. The details relating to the bread and cup are interesting and stand in various relations to the other accounts of the Last Supper in the synoptic Gospels (cf. Matt. 26:26–29; Mark 14:22–25; Luke 22:14–23), but need not detain us here.

More important is what Paul has to say about the meaning of the eucharistic gathering and how it should be approached. First, the practice of eating bread and drinking blood at the eucharist is fundamentally eschatological; it is connected by Paul with the death of Jesus and his return at the end of the age (v. 26). Second, to eat and drink at this gathering unworthily is a profanity; self-examination must precede participation (v. 28). Paul's reference to "the body" in verse 29 is a reference to the image he will use of the community in 12:12–31 (cf. 10:16–17). It is here that Paul's key concern emerges: division and disorder at the eucharist will bring judgment upon the participants. The ambiguity here as to whether "the body" refers to the body of Christ at the eucharist or the body of Christ the church is probably intentional. The food of the eucharist and the body of the community of the church must be seen together. The reference to some having become weak and ill and dying through abuse of the eucharist is a particularly sobering reminder of the power of the eucharist and its significance in the community (v. 30).

Paul is not here concerned with human or worldly judgment but with the judgment of God. The judgment of the Lord, Paul says, is a chastening experience whose opposite is condemnation (vv. 31, 32). Paul indicates that when they come together to celebrate the eucharist and eat their food, the Corinthians must wait for each other. The combination in these verses of a highly charged eschatology rooted in the death of Jesus, and judgment if the occasion is not spiritually and practically orderly, indicates Paul's conviction that the body of the community and the body of Christ can only be built up where the members consider others before themselves. The emphasis here, once again, is on "discerning the body."

What, then, is the connection between food, conscience, and the eucharist in 1 Corinthians? The significance of food and relationships arising out of eating together are not always appreciated by readers of Paul's letters. Clearly when it came to the practical question of whether Jewish and Gentile Christians needed to worry about their past religious requirements in terms of food, the answer was not so straightforward for the Corinthian Christians or for Paul himself. The Corinthians had belonged to different religions before coming to Christ and had brought different expectations and practices with them into the community. The bottom line for Paul was that food itself was not an important issue, but rather how people actually related to other members of the Christian community.

The word "conscience" (*suneidesis*) is difficult to interpret, but it is clear that a wide variety of meanings can be found for it in many different contexts. In Second Temple Judaism and therefore also in Paul's day, this word had more to do with feelings arising after an incident than with a guiding principle determining an action. It also developed to concern relations with other people. In 1 Corinthians it clearly concerns relations with others, and Paul relates the issue of food closely to that of conscience. It is not a question of whether it is right or wrong to eat food sacrificed to idols but of whether anyone in the community might be led astray and think that other gods must therefore exist and can be worshipped. In order to build up the community of the church, Paul advises that people's behavior be modified in relation to others.

Although Paul doesn't use the word "conscience" in 1 Corinthians 11, his message concerning the eucharist is basically the same. It is in this way seen as simply another, though very special (it is the *Lord*'s supper, cf. verse 20) sort of food.

The breakdown in community relations in Corinth and the division among those present at the eucharist could only be healed by "discerning the body," that is, by taking into account the needs and concerns of others before one's own needs. In all this, food, conscience, and the eucharist are fundamentally related for Paul as he attempts to build up the body of Christ in Corinth.

SIX

PAUL AND WOMEN
SETTING THE RECORD
STRAIGHT

Paul's attitude to women has been the subject of considerable debate in the last century or so. As is well known, he
has usually been portrayed as largely negative in this
respect: his understanding of marriage and sex, for example, seems
rather limited, and his teaching on women's roles in Christian
worship looks negative and contradictory. And yet Paul worked
with a significant number of women and seems to have greatly
valued their ministries. How realistic, then, is the usual understanding of Paul, and does it do justice to his real struggle with
particular individuals and specific practical needs?

In fact, when we look closely at the relevant passages in Paul's
letters, the usual picture is quickly modified. Most of the recent
discussions about Paul and women have arisen in historical-crit-
ical and feminist circles. There have been those who have simply
wished to know "what Paul really said" on particular issues, and
who have tried to reconstruct his original context and message.
There have also been feminist theologians and New Testament
scholars who have reread Paul's letters paying particular attention
to women, and who have noted how women have often been
read out of the story, ignored, or even interpreted as men. In both
areas, the popular picture of Paul's attitude to women has been
shown to be inadequate and misleading. This is not to deny that

Paul lived at a time and in a culture in which women were largely second-class citizens or that he can suddenly be seen as the father of gender equality. But it is clear that with a better understanding of his historical context and with some of the later misogynist interpretations of his letters erased, Paul soon emerges in a significantly different light.

In this chapter I first show something of the extent of Paul's involvement with women and their significance in his life and ministry; second, I discuss the comments he makes about women in 1 Corinthians 11 and 14; and finally, I examine Galatians 3:28 to see to what extent this indicates a theological context in which Paul's comments about women might be seen.

Women in Paul's Life

Before turning specifically to passages in which Paul has something to say about women, it is worth noting the women with whom Paul came into contact. In the wake of the view that Paul was somehow "against women" it is often assumed that he had little to do with them, but nothing could be further from the truth: there are a number of significant women with whom Paul worked or with whom he came into contact in some way in the communities in which he moved. Of course, the range of women that might be mentioned here as having come into contact with Paul depends on the sources that are to be used when looking for them. Obviously there will be more women if all the letters attributed to Paul in the New Testament are used, in addition to the Acts of the Apostles. If we include only the authentically Pauline letters, there will be fewer. Some women are mentioned both in letters and in the Acts. Even if we were to count only the women mentioned in Paul's own letters, however, it would be clear that women played a significant role in his life.

It is worth noting first just how women have been erased from Paul's life by later interpretation. The most blatant case of this is Junia in Romans 16:7. This person's name in Greek is Iounian and could in principle be either male or female. For centuries this person was, in fact, understood to be a woman and it seems likely that she was. In the last century, however, she became known as Junias instead of Junia and was suddenly understood to be a man. In a dramatic reinterpretation, one of the women in Paul's life was eliminated. Junia was an apostle (*apostolos*) in the church in Rome (although the Greek could simply mean known among the apostles) and known to Paul himself.

In realizing that women have been eliminated from Paul's life in the past, commentators are now much more careful to note them when they appear. The following are the most important: Phoebe, a deaconess (*diakonos*) in the church in Rome (Rom. 16:1), although she seems to have had more responsibility than the modern use of this word suggests; Euodia and Syntyche, co-workers (*sunergon*) with Paul in Philippi (Phil. 4:2); Prisca, another co-worker in Rome and Corinth (Rom. 16:3; 1 Cor. 16:19); and Chloe, the leader of the group in Corinth who kept in touch with Paul after he had departed and told him of the splits in the community (1 Cor. 1:11). In the final chapter of Romans, among many greetings, Paul mentions other workers (*kopian*) in the church there: Mary (Rom. 16:6); Tryphaena, Tryphosa, and Persis (v. 12); the mother of Rufus (v. 13); and Julia and the sister of Nereus (v. 15). Paul's letter to Philemon is also addressed to Apphia (Philemon v. 2). If we include the women mentioned in Acts and the deutero-Pauline letters, the list extends to a few more: Lois and Eunice (2 Tim. 1:5; cf. Acts 16:1); Damaris (Acts 17:34); and Lydia (Acts 16:11–40); in addition to other key women who are part of Paul's story, such as Drusilla and Bernice, although they are much less significant (Acts 24:24; 25:13). The overall picture, then, is that there were a number of significant women in Paul's life and that he worked willingly with them on a regular basis. What was his attitude to them and to their ministries?

1 Corinthians 11 and 14

Two key passages present themselves for discussion here. They concern Paul's attitude to women's roles in worship in the church in Corinth. Other material that often features in discussions of Paul's attitude to women is probably not in fact by him (i.e., Eph. 5:22–33; 1 Tim. 2:11–15). The two key passages are 1 Corinthians 11:2–16 and 14:34–36. These passages are important in what they say individually and also because they appear to contradict each other. Both have been used to support the view that Paul was negative about women, but in fact this interpretation is based on a very naïve understanding of the passages and their contexts. Let us look at them in turn.

(a) 1 Corinthians 11:2–16

The first passage is popularly perceived to be about women wearing veils during worship. It seems to suggest that women are subordinate to men in their role in worship and in creation. Certainly Paul inherited a culture and a theology in which women were subordinate to men. The problem with the popular interpretation of this passage is that the other elements in the picture are often obscured. What Paul has to say is rooted in a theology of creation in which everything, including men, is subordinate to Christ and to God. Paul's understanding of creation is rooted in the notion of a hierarchy beginning with God at the top, Christ second, man third, and woman fourth. Each one is headed by the one above. In this sense everyone has a role in creation under God, and it is not a matter of one lording it over another. After all, Christ is the head of man, and God of Christ. This is the context in which Paul sets what he has to say about women (11:2–3).

But we must also note the wider context within the church in Corinth. It is possible that there was a practice in Corinth of women not veiling their heads to pray and prophesy. Commentators have discussed the background situation in detail here, and some have suggested that there might have been a movement of radical women in Corinth who sought their own liberation through not wearing veils. Although this is disputed, it is clear that there were at least some women praying and prophesying without veils and that this had become a problem in the community. Paul writes to offer his advice on the matter. He speaks of creation, authority, and glory and uses the metaphor of the "head" to link human beings to God.

The first element in the argument is that if a man prays or prophesies with his head (*kephale*) covered, he dishonors his head. The heart of the argument lies in the word "head" here. It obviously means the physical head of the man, but we have already been told that a man's head is Christ. The dishonoring, therefore, is of both himself and Christ. In the same way the woman who prays and prophesies with her head *un*covered dishonors her head, which is both her own physical head and also man. At this point the argument turns on a feature of Paul's culture: men have short hair and women long. Paul understands this to be written in creation (v. 14). Thus, if a woman prays without a veil it is the same as if she shaves her head; it is dishonorable (11:6). So far so good, although one may take issue with Paul over the basic premise. Next, Paul alludes to Genesis 1:26–27 when he claims that man is made in the image and glory of God. Woman is excluded from the picture here, but the emphasis is now on image and glory in the context of creation. Once again, man's not covering his head is part of this: he reflects the glory of God (and by implication Christ). Now the Genesis story of creation is specifically referred to when Paul mentions woman being made from the side of man (Gen. 2:18–25). Clearly, woman is subordinate to man, but the real emphasis is on their different roles in creation under Christ and God.

Whatever we make of the argument based on the length of hair, the head covering is the key element. The problem here is made even more difficult by the fact that in verse 10 Paul's Greek says a woman should have *exousia* on her head. This word has usually been translated "veil," but its basic meaning is "authority." Why would Paul claim that a woman should have authority on her head? It is possible that an Aramaic word (*sltwnyh*) links both meanings: veil and authority. But in any case, the word used earlier in the passage is *kalumma* and means veil. It is clear that the head covering has to do with the glory which the women reflects, that of man, and also with a certain sort of authority which she has.

The next part of verse 10 complicates the issue even more. Paul says that woman ought to have *exousia* on her head "because of the angels." A variety of explanations of this phrase have been put forward. Are these angels evil angels who might prey upon the women in the community worship, like the sons of god of Genesis 6:2 who swept away whichever of them they desired? Does Paul mean that the angels in the heavenly court themselves wore veils out of reverence for God (perhaps recalling Is. 6) and that women should do the same? In some passages in the Dead Sea Scrolls it is said that anyone with a physical defect should be excluded from the community worship because they were considered less than whole and might be offensive to God or the angels. Could it be that women who have no veil (just as if they had no hair) would be considered physically less than perfect and therefore offensive to the angels? The meaning of this verse remains obscure.

In the next verse Paul is quick to remind his readers of the real structure of relations in creation. Women and men are interrelated and interdependent in the Lord. Woman might have been made from man in Genesis, but men are born of women ever after. For Paul, everything comes from God, and both men and women in their respective roles need to remember their "heads."

What does all this tell us about Paul's attitude to women? Although there are some difficult phrases to unravel here, Paul follows the basic Jewish notion from Genesis and elsewhere that men and women have different roles in creation. Both women and men play their respective roles in creation under God. But why then should women wear veils? Morna Hooker has put forward an explanation of this passage that makes a good deal of sense. In the context of creation and worship, she says, men are uncovered because their "head" is Christ and they reflect the glory of God. Women cover up because their head is man and they do not wish to reflect his glory but that of God. Men and women thus both reflect the glory of God in worship, but in different ways and in line with their different places in creation.

Whatever we make of the various complexities in this passage, Paul is obviously saying that women must be veiled when they pray or prophesy. There is no question in his mind that women *should* pray and prophesy even if only when inspired by the spirit. There is, therefore, no prohibition of women's participation in worship as such, and Paul's attitude is positive. All this is fully in line with what we know from elsewhere about Paul's attitude to the women he encountered and worked with. Why is it, then, that in 1 Corinthians 14 Paul seems to be saying that women must be silent in church?

(b) 1 Corinthians 14:34–36

The second passage that concerns us here is often cited to support the view that Paul is negative about women and women's ministry. It is a passage that seems to be saying that the women of Corinth should be quiet in church. It is then assumed that this is Paul's considered view of women and their ministries in general, especially as he says that this is the practice "in all the churches" (14:34). He also says that "it is shameful for a woman to speak in church" (v. 35) and that women are subordinate to men (v. 34). As far as church is concerned, he says, the women can ask their husbands about what is going on when they get home! On the face of it, this passage seems to contradict 1 Corinthians 11:2–16, and some commentators have concluded that it was not written by Paul at all but was added later. The fact that the passage is also a textual variant and is absent from some of the early manuscripts of 1 Corinthians has complicated the debates about its place in Paul's thinking. However, there are other matters to consider in interpreting this passage. In looking more closely at Paul's own context here it becomes clear that this is a specific passage directed at specific people and is not out of harmony with what Paul says elsewhere. It is important to look at the wider context of the passage, that is, the rest of 1 Corinthians 14, if we are to see its full significance. It is worth noting, first of all, one line from the passage itself: in verse 35 Paul says of the Corinthian women in question, "let them ask their husbands at home." This indicates that this passage is first of all about married women rather than all women. Also, when the whole chapter is taken into account it is clear that the context concerns "speaking in tongues" and prophesying and is not about women or women's ministry per se. It is about a particular group of married, tongue-speaking, charismatic women in Corinth at the time of Paul.

The context of 1 Corinthians 14:34–36 shows that Paul has been dealing with speaking in tongues and prophecy. These have also been Paul's concern in 1 Corinthians 12 where he writes, "Now concerning spiritual gifts" (12:1) and then goes on to deal with the different gifts of those in the body of Christ, an image he also uses later in the chapter (vv. 12–31). The great "song to love" of 1 Corinthians 13 falls in the center of Paul's teaching on gifts, and then chapter 14 focuses on tongue-speaking and prophecy, with Paul's familiar emphasis on building up the community (vv. 3, 12).

Clearly there were spiritual gifts and "speaking in tongues" in the church in Corinth, and this has been one of the things that has come up as a problem with which Paul has to deal (cf. 7:1; 8:1; 12:1). By way of controlling a situation in which there seems to have been considerable charismatic experience and expression, Paul emphasizes that he wishes to see interpretation as well as tongue-speaking. In fact, he says that he would rather speak five words with his mind than ten thousand in a tongue (14:19). Paul is affirming order in charismatic worship and tells the Corinthians that the members must take their turn to speak in tongues (14:27). If there is no interpreter, then everyone is to be silent as far as tongues are concerned. The same is to be the case with the prophets. The emphasis in all this is on peace and order, and on real inspiration by the spirit in worship that has apparently become overly charismatic and disorderly. It is in this context in 1 Corinthians 14 that the passage concerning women occurs.

The English translations of 1 Corinthians can be misleading. Very often in the present passage we have the word "women," but the Greek word Paul uses here is *gune*, a word that can be translated "wife" as well as "woman." In verse 35 these *gunai* are to "ask their husbands at home" if they want to know anything, and the translation here should clearly be "wives." We are thus dealing with the married women of Corinth in a particular situation regarding speaking in tongues and prophesying.

Paul certainly saw women as having a different role in creation from men (cf. 1 Cor. 11 and 1 Tim. 2:11–15), but in 1 Corinthians 14 Paul is not speaking about all women and it is not because they are women that they are silenced by Paul, but because they are particular tongue-speakers who are not truly inspired by the spirit and who are disrupting the worship. It is as important for Paul that any disrupters be silent (vv. 28, 30). He is not writing down his view of women for posterity, but, as always, is writing to a particular group of people about some women. This understanding of this passage leaves 1 Corinthians 14:34–36 relative to very specific circumstances in first-century Corinth. With the broader picture in mind, it can be seen that this passage does not contradict the directions of 1 Corinthians 11. It is simply addressed to different women in a different situation. Paul is happy when women who are truly inspired by the spirit pray and prophesy, but not when some particular women disrupt worship. Once again, in the light of this the popular perception of Paul's "attitude to women" looks naïve and uninformed. He is much more positive than that.

Galatians 3:28

We turn finally to a text that might give us an idea of what Paul's overall attitude to women was. Galatians 3:28 reads, "There is neither Jew nor Greek, there is neither slave nor free, there is neither male nor female" (cf. 1 Cor. 12:12–13). Possibly originally a baptismal formula, this text has been interpreted in a variety of conflicting ways. The context is no longer Corinth but the church in Galatia, and we must be careful here as before not to assume that Paul is stating a universal principle. However, there are significant differences here as Paul is saying something about the results of what he believes has happened overall in Christ. There has, he believes, been a "new creation" (Gal. 6:15; cf. 2 Cor. 5:17; Col. 3:10). The letter is addressed to a church that was riddled with difficulties regarding the place of the Jewish past in the light of the new experience of Christ, and this forms the context of what he has to say.

There are three dimensions: first, Jews and Greeks have been brought into a new context and the old inequalities have been removed. Second, social differences between slave and free have been transcended and both now stand in the same position before God. And finally, this element of newness in Christ extends to the level of gender. What has happened in Christ has affected inequalities between male and female. The usual translation, "there is neither male nor female," however, is technically incorrect when we look closely at Paul's Greek; it should read "there is no longer male *and* female." Paul's point is more than that the two distinct genders are now equal, but that "male and female" together are transcended by the new creation in Christ. The verse recalls Genesis 1:26–27, which refers to the creation of male and female. If Paul thinks that the male-female relation is no longer constitutive of the identity of individuals, that all are now equal in creation, and that all inequalities are transcended in Christ, then he possibly also thinks that male and female still have distinct and different roles in the new creation. It is also possible that the equality of male and female which Paul states in Galatians 3:28 has an eschatological aspect and has not yet become reality at the practical level in the Pauline communities. This would then explain the remaining differences in practice. Either way, Galatians 3:28 indicates that Paul's attitude to women is fundamentally positive and that the popular portrayal of his views as negative is misleading.

When we look closely at Paul's letters and the contexts into which he wrote, it is clear that he is not as negative about women as is often made out. Rather than having a negative attitude to women and their ministries, Paul worked with a number of women and valued them highly. Feminist theologians and historians of Christianity have helped to draw attention to just how many women there were in Paul's life and how they have often been ignored. Passages that are often cited to show that Paul was against women look very different when they are seen in their original contexts. One of the key mistakes is to suppose that Paul is making universal statements for all time instead of writing a specific letter to a specific community. Also, words in Paul's letters that have been translated into English in a particular way often conceal ambiguities and alternatives that are important and bear upon Paul's actual meaning. All of this should make us at least wary of pronouncing on Paul's attitude to women and their ministries before we have looked closely at his real situation.

In the first two passages we have looked at here, Paul is addressing specific occasions in Corinth. One has to do with head coverings, which are explainable in terms of the theology of creation and glory on which Paul is operating. The other is very specific, and is aimed at a particular group of charismatic women in Corinth, and is really about order in worship. There is, of course, no doubt that Paul as a man of his age followed the culture and theology of his day regarding women. But his emphasis was on different roles in creation under God and Christ rather than on subordination and inequality in the negative sense. Galatians 3:28 does give a hint of where Paul's theology of gender lies: male and female are distinct but equal in Christ. In the light of this, reinterpreting these two Pauline passages as we have done here makes perfect sense, and Paul's "attitude to women" can be seen to be far less negative and far more subtle and specific than is often supposed.

SEVEN

PAUL AND
HOMOSEXUALITY
WHAT'S THE PROBLEM?

A number of serious difficulties arise early on in a consideration of Paul's attitude to homosexuality. First, the word itself has a wide range of meanings and is understood in different ways by different people in different contexts. Elements in a whole range of sexual activities and relationships between men might be in mind when this word is used, and it is often quite unclear exactly what is meant. Anything from uncommitted promiscuity and prostitution to committed lifelong relationships might be the subject when the word "homosexuality" is used, and contemporary debates about the legitimacy or otherwise of such relationships are bedeviled by this ambiguity.

Second, the word "homosexuality" was only invented in the nineteenth century, and there is no biblical Hebrew or Greek equivalent. One needs to be particularly careful, therefore, to be clear what one is talking about; the potential for anachronism is considerable. And third, the notion that individuals have a particular sexual "disposition" or "orientation" seems to be relatively recent. This inevitably adds to the complexity of the debate about what homosexuality is and what Paul thought about it.

More serious still, perhaps, is the fact that although modern discussions about homosexuality, especially in the churches, tend to focus on committed lifelong relationships between two males, there isn't any evidence that these were widespread in the ancient world, and Paul never seems to have been confronted by them. He certainly has some negative things to say about sex between men, but he is most likely referring to male prostitution rather than committed long-term relationships.

Paul's words have been used in recent debates to encourage the condemnation of homosexuality, but the things he says come from a very different cultural context from our own, and his words have often been translated into English inadequately. All these difficulties contribute to making the task of addressing "Paul and homosexuality" complex and often inconclusive.

The main task in this chapter is to try to determine the original context of the few things Paul says about this subject and to discern exactly what it was he objected to. An important part of this is to find out what the various attitudes to sexual relations between males were in the ancient world and to consider how Paul's views were influenced by them. So I first consider attitudes to sexual relationships between males in ancient Greece and Rome; second, I discuss the relevant texts in the Hebrew Bible; and third, I examine the Pauline texts that refer to sexual activity between males.

Homosexuality and the Greco-Roman World

It is well known that attitudes to sexual relations between males in ancient Greece and Rome were very different from what they are in most cultures today. For a start, people didn't think in terms of the "sexual orientation" of individuals in the way they do now, and there is no evidence of the formal categories of homosexuality, heterosexuality, and bisexuality as we think of them today (unless, as we shall see, one thinks of "bisexuality" as somehow being the norm). Instead, there existed an "active-passive" polarity evident in the different roles people played in society. This was reflected in sexual relations in which men usually had an active role and women a passive role. This basic dynamic had to do with power and supremacy over weakness and submission rather than with individual sexual orientation. In ancient Greece and Rome there is literary and other evidence (e.g., wall paintings and vases) that sex between two males was perfectly acceptable in principle, one active and the other passive.

It is worth noting that an ideal of male beauty dominated ancient Greece in the same way that female beauty dominates many societies today. Male nakedness was widely accepted, and in some places young men exercised in the nude in the gymnasiums. Ancient Greece and Rome were both "male-dominated" societies and sexual relations with women were thought of in terms of procreation rather than friendship and love, which could best be found with a male partner. There is far less evidence of sexual relationships between women in Greek culture than between men, although they clearly existed, as the love poetry of Sappho of Lesbos shows.

Within the general context of sex between males being accepted in ancient Greece the practice of pederasty was widely known, especially among the upper classes of society. In this, an older male (Greek: *erastes*, lover) formed a relationship with a younger male (Greek: *eromenos*, beloved). Usually this happened around the time of the boy's puberty. Pederasty was not "homosexuality" as such, and was not in principle based upon sex although it did include sex. At its heart it was more a spiritual friendship focused on social training. The older male would be a friend and mentor to the younger male, providing an example as a teacher or guide in growth toward adulthood. Most males would eventually marry, and their relationships with their male lovers would usually but not always cease. Cases in which a relationship between two males lasted for a longer period and excluded marriage are few and far between.

As in relationships between men and women, pederasty operated on an active-passive polarity, the older male taking an active role and the younger male a passive role. This meant that the power dynamic that prevailed between men and women also prevailed between men and boys. Although it was respectable for an older male to have younger male lovers, the younger male was somewhat disgraced by this relationship in that he was put into the passive role of a woman. His aim was to grow up and find his own lovers, thus becoming sexually active and socially dominant himself. There were different kinds of pederastic relations between males involving different ages and roles, but the basic model prevailed in most cases.

In Rome the situation was similar but with some differences. Sexual relationships between males were very common and were generally accepted as part of the social landscape of the culture, although they were perhaps not quite as prevalent as in Greece. Men had sexual relationships with young boys, and many of these were between masters and slaves. Sex between freemen was less common and was considered less proper. The key difference between Greece and Rome was that the Greek idea of pederasty with its "training for adulthood" was absent in Roman society. The relations were much more sexual in their basic concept in Rome. However, a similar active-passive dynamic operated, and the passive partner was seen as shameful because he had taken the submissive, passive role of a woman. As in Greece, all this took place in a culture in which sexual relations with women were seen as primarily for purposes of procreation. Friendships and relationships with men were seen as superior, and in terms of modern categories many males would appear to have been "bisexual."

In spite of occasional criticisms of sexual relationships between males from some philosophers in both Greece and Rome on the grounds that they were "unnatural" (*para phusin*: "against nature") because there was no resulting procreation, such relationships were generally accepted. They were not considered deviant or perverse. However, as might be expected in such circumstances, there was a good deal of promiscuity and rape, and many effeminate young men sold their bodies in prostitution to older males for financial and material gain. In this context relationships between older and younger males often didn't last long: the older male would move on to another "beloved" and the younger male would end up physically and emotionally abused. As we shall see later, it is this most visible dimension of sex between males in Greek society to which Paul seems to object.

Homosexuality and Ancient Judaism

The attitude to sex between males found in ancient Judaism is very different from that in ancient Greece and Rome. There are only a few relevant texts in the Hebrew Bible, and although these are often taken as evidence that homosexuality was condemned in ancient Israel, the picture is far less clear than that. The texts concerned are as follows. First, the creation narrative in Genesis 1 and 2. This is often used in arguments against homosexuality, but the passage never mentions same-sex relationships and doesn't positively condemn them. Second, the story of Ham and Noah in Genesis 9:20–27. Ham "sees his father naked" in this story, which in Hebrew probably means that he had sexual intercourse with him. However, the sex in the story indicates power and domination and isn't itself the focus of concern.

Third is the story of Sodom and Gomorrah in Genesis 19:1–29. Here the men of the town wish to "get to know" (Hebrew: *yada*) the visitors. The Hebrew word can mean "to have intercourse with" and although it certainly doesn't always mean this, it could mean it here. In any case, it is not the sex that is condemned in this story but the lack of hospitality shown by the inhabitants of Sodom to the visitors (the main theme of Gen. 18 is hospitality). The threatened sex actually looks more like male rape than anything else, and the story's real emphasis is power and domination rather than sex as such (cf. the rape of the Levite's concubine in Judges 19:1–30). Some scholars maintain that this story was not seen as being about homosexuality until very much later. The biblical texts that mention Sodom and Gomorrah, they claim, do not draw attention to sexual activity between males as the cause for judgment, although this is perhaps not always clear (cf. Deut. 29:23; 32:32; Is. 1:9–10; 13:19; Jer. 49:18; Lam. 4:6; Ezek. 16:46–50; Amos 4:11; Zeph. 2:9; Matt. 10:15 // Luke 10:12; Matt. 11:23–24; Luke 17:28–29; 2 Peter 2:6; Jude 7; Rev. 11:8; and the writings of many of the early church fathers, e.g., Origen, Ambrose, and John Cassian).

Fourth are the references to prostitutes in Deuteronomy 23:17–18. It is not exactly clear what sort of prostitutes these were, but again power and domination through sex, rather than the sex itself, are the key emphases. Even if these stories are seen to be about sex, they are clearly more about rape than about other kinds of relationships between males.

Fifth, Leviticus 18:22 and 20:13: the first text says "You shall not lie with a male as with a woman; it is an abomination" (RSV). The condemnation comes in a list of things that are an "abomination" (which really means an "impurity," Hebrew: *toevah*), such as sexual intercourse with a woman during her menstrual period, or with a neighbor's wife, child sacrifice, and sexual intercourse with an animal. The second text is even more serious and recommends the death penalty: "If a man lies with a male as with a woman, both of them have committed an abomination; they shall be put to death, their blood is upon them" (RSV). The context of both texts is the so-called Holiness Code of Leviticus 17–26, whose focus is purity for the Israelites in the face of the idolatrous practices of foreigners. It is possible that the views expressed in these texts are related in some way to temple prostitutes, but it is more likely that the practices are forbidden because they are simply "what foreigners do" and are therefore impure. Rather than focusing on sex as such, these texts, taken alongside the rest of the code, are about purity, power, domination—and gender roles within that context. What is condemned is most likely to be male prostitution as found in other nations.

The final relevant texts in the Hebrew Bible are 1 Samuel 18–20 and 2 Samuel 1:26 and concern the famous relationship between David and Jonathan (not unrelated, perhaps, to similar examples of heroic same-sex love in ancient Greek mythology and history). These have actually been used to argue in favor of homosexuality. It is probable that the relationship between David and Jonathan should be understood simply as a deep personal friendship with no physical sexual content. But even though sex is never mentioned explicitly in the story, the texts could be read as implying it. Whatever the truth is, David and Jonathan provide an example of a loving relationship between two men that is affirmed by a biblical writer. As an aside, it is interesting to note here that there is no evidence of lesbianism in the Hebrew Bible, and it is unclear whether this was unknown in ancient Israel or was simply considered unspeakable.

In the light of the foregoing discussion it can be seen that there were different attitudes to sexual relations between males in ancient Greece and Rome on the one hand and in ancient Israel on the other. But overall, there is little evidence of "homosexuality" as an individual orientation or as a committed, long-term relationship between two males—or of these being condemned. Much of the sex that is referred to looks more like rape and prostitution than anything else and involves power, manipulation, and the domination of one person by another. In light of this we now turn specifically to what Paul, who was influenced by all these cultures, has to say about sex between males.

Paul and Homosexuality

The first thing to consider in this section is Paul's general approach to sex. There have been many different readings of Paul's outlook on sex but a few basic points are worth making. Paul doesn't give us a detailed account of what he thinks about sex per se. Even so, some of the things he does say indicate fairly clearly what his concerns are. In 1 Corinthians 7 Paul seems to see marriage and sex, even between men and women, as a concession. His comment in 7:9 that "it is better to marry than to be aflame with passion" certainly gives this impression. He also says that it is better to remain single as he does (v. 8). The basic outlook, however, is that marriage and sex are a distraction in an age when the end of time is coming; celibacy is much more appropriate. Nevertheless, within marriage, sex is to be treated fairly and partners are to respect each other's needs, although they can also have times of restraint.

All this is important because the situation to which Paul wrote in ancient Corinth was one in which, by all accounts, prostitution and the abuse of sex were rife. Paul's comments on sex between married people and his ideal of celibacy must also therefore be seen in the context of the things Paul really disapproved of: promiscuity, prostitution, and rape. It is the misuse and abuse of sex that Paul condemns most of all.

With this in mind we now turn to the few comments about sex between males that Paul makes. The attitudes that we have discussed from ancient Greece, Rome, and Israel all play into what he has to say, and he must have been aware of a wide range of approaches and practices. The three relevant texts are as follows: Romans 1:26–27; 1 Corinthians 6:9; and 1 Timothy 1:10. First Timothy was probably not written by Paul himself but is interesting because of the light it might shed on a Greek word Paul uses in 1 Corinthians 6:9.

The first relevant text is Romans 1:26–27. In the first part of this letter Paul writes to the Romans about the sinfulness of humanity and of God's offer of salvation in Jesus Christ. The important words are as follows:

> For this reason God gave them up to dishonourable passions. Their women exchanged natural relations for unnatural, and the men likewise gave up natural relations with women and were consumed with passion for one another, men committing shameless acts with men and receiving in their own persons the due penalty for their error. (RSV)

We have no indication of any specific background to these words or whether Paul had any individuals or particular practices in mind. His wider message in Romans 1, however, is crucial: in its sinfulness, the human race has become idolatrous, worshipping the creation instead of the creator (v. 25). The list of vices that Paul gives in later verses (28–32) includes some of the symptoms of this idolatry. The sexual sins he names are part of this generally idolatrous condition. Idolatry and sexual sins were related elsewhere in ancient literature and Paul seems to know of this (cf. Wisd. of Sol. 14:12). Apparently both men and women had "exchanged natural relations" (v. 26) where sexual activity is concerned, although we hear no more from Paul about sexual relations between females. The key question here is what Paul means by "natural" (Greek: *phusis*). The Greek word for "nature" is complex, but to Paul it would have meant something more like a cultural rule, practice, or convention than something biological in the modern sense. The idea of "nature" for Paul was different from that of "creation" (Greek: *ktisis*), which he does not refer to here; nor does he refer to the Genesis creation narrative. All of this indicates that Paul does not think that any "laws of nature" are being broken through this change of practice. Rather, both women and men have given up their natural relations and exchanged the usual conventional practice for another practice, and this is idolatrous. Many commentators argue that Paul seems not to be thinking of those that are "homosexually oriented," as we would say today, but rather of those that are "heterosexual" but have changed their practice. In the context of a condemnation of idolatry, Paul is condemning behavior that abuses and exploits people and is not their usual and "natural" practice.

The second relevant Pauline text is 1 Corinthians 6:9: "Do not be deceived; neither the immoral, nor idolaters, nor adulterers, nor *homosexuals*, nor thieves, nor the greedy, nor drunkards, nor revilers, nor robbers will inherit the kingdom of God" (RSV). We have already noted the context of prostitution and promiscuity in ancient Corinth in the time of Paul. This list of vices (cf. 1 Cor. 5:10f.) might have been taken over by Paul from somewhere else, but it must now be seen in its Corinthian context. The immediate problem here is that whereas many recent English translations have the word "homosexuals," "sexual perverts" or some variant of this, the actual Greek that Paul wrote involves two words whose meaning is not wholly clear: *malakoi* and *arsenokoitai*. It is the word *arsenokoitai* that is also used at 1 Timothy 1:10 in another similar list of vices. It is important to examine the meaning of these two words in order to see to what Paul is really objecting. The word *malakos* probably means "soft" and may be used in a variety of contexts with different meanings relating, for example, to illness or some sort of physical weakness. It also means "effeminacy" and is sometimes used of the boy partner in a Greek pederastic relationship. However, the word was not always used in relation to sex and we cannot assume that it always had a sexual meaning.

The second word, *arsenokoitai*, is even more difficult to translate. It seems that Paul was the first person to use this word so there isn't anything to go on in terms of finding the background meaning. Clearly the first part of the word *arsen* means "male" and *koite* means a "bed." The meaning, then, is clearly sexual although what particular act it refers to is unclear. Does it refer to someone who sleeps with men? Or to a man who sleeps with others, perhaps male and female? Some scholars have claimed that the word refers to male prostitutes, others, that it means the active partner in a same-sex relationship. Others still have claimed that the two words *malakoi* and *arsenokoitai* refer to the active and passive partners in Greek pederastic relationship, but this narrows the meanings of the words far too much and seems unlikely. On the contrary, it is clear that the words have broad meanings that can only be determined from the context in which they are used. Paul certainly gives no context for the individual elements in his list of vices and does not spell out exactly what he is condemning. It is clear that the second word, *arsenokoitai*, includes reference to sexual activity between males and as such this is certainly condemned by Paul.

Though 1 Timothy was probably not written by Paul, the occurrence of *arsenokoitai* in that text is worth some attention. In

1 Timothy 1:10, as in 1 Corinthians 6:9, the word occurs in a list of vices. The author is referring to general lawlessness and lists three vices, among others, that shed light upon each other and are probably not inconsistent with Paul's own views. The three vices are *pornos*, *arsenokoitai*, and *andrapodistai*. The first, *pornos*, is the word frequently used for a male prostitute, although this can also be used much more widely to mean immorality generally. The last word, *andrapodistais*, means "kidnappers" or "slave dealers." It is possible that these other two words fill out the background of the middle word *arsenokoitai* and suggest that this is indeed associated (at least here) with male prostitution and with the sexual use and abuse of slaves. If abusive sex between males is being suggested here in 1 Timothy, it might well be that this is what Paul is condemning when he uses the word *arsenokoitai* in 1 Corinthians.

In discussing the few relevant Pauline texts and their backgrounds, it can be seen that Paul would have known of Greek pederasty and of the Jewish condemnation of sex between males. He would have been aware of the abuse that went on in some sexual relationships between males. He would certainly have been shocked by the behavior of young male prostitutes on the streets of the cities in which he preached the Gospel. Among the many different things that the word "homosexuality" might mean today it is clearly promiscuity, prostitution, and rape that Paul condemns rather than committed, loving relationships between males.

The word "homosexuality" refers to a whole range of different relationships and activities between men. In Paul's world it did not indicate a specific category of sexual orientation. In the cultures of ancient Greece and Rome sex between males was certainly well known and largely accepted. The system of pederasty was particularly well established, and if anything the general male outlook of the day was probably closer to what we would now think of as "bisexuality" than to anything else. Within that context there was a great deal of promiscuity, prostitution, and rape. It was probably this element in the whole thing that provoked the disapproval of some of the philosophers of the day. From ancient Israel, the texts of the Hebrew Bible that refer to sex between males have been interpreted in a variety of different ways. They have often been used in arguments against homosexuality, but on closer inspection cannot be seen to be concerned with homosexuality as a condition. Most of the texts refer to particular instances of male prostitution or rape, and in any case they are often not primarily about the sex that occurs in them but rather about social power, domination, and religious impurity.

When we turn to Paul we must take into account these Greco-Roman and Jewish backgrounds. Paul would probably have been very familiar with many different practices and attitudes where sex occurred between males. He would have known the system of pederasty from Greece; he would have known of sex between masters and slaves in Rome; and he would have been aware of the condemnations of prostitution or male rape in the Torah. Paul would have known, perhaps in detail, of the abuses of sex in places like ancient Corinth and would have been aware of promiscuity, prostitution, and rape among men. As a Jew, he must have been shocked by the behavior of male prostitutes who sold their bodies on the streets of ancient Corinth for material and financial gain, and there is no doubt that he condemned such things.

But as far as we know, Paul never encountered any cases of two males attempting a committed, loving relationship.

His comments, therefore, have little relevance to modern debates about such matters. Even so, it can be seen that Paul's condemnation of male prostitution no more condemns all homosexuality at all times than his condemnation of abusive male-female sexual relations condemns all heterosexuality at all times. And given Paul's disapproval of abusive sexual relationships between males, it is reasonable to surmise that his general outlook might have been more sympathetic to respectful, committed, loving relationships between males than is often made out: though, of course, it is strictly impossible to speculate on what someone might think if they had lived in cultures that they never imagined!

EIGHT

A REVOLUTION IN PAULINE STUDIES

CONSIDERING THE "NEW LOOK" ON PAUL

For several centuries now, scholars, commentators, and Christians generally have interpreted Paul and his theology in a particular way. The dominant view has looked something like this: Paul believed that the creator God of Israel had called a people to himself and established a covenant with them issuing in the Torah. In time, Israel became arrogant, boastful, and legalistic, and Judaism became a religion of works-righteousness in which Jews thought that if they kept the precepts of the law impeccably they could earn God's favor and establish their own salvation. In view of this, God decided that he must establish an alternative religion of pure grace and forgiveness. He sent his son Jesus Christ, whose death and resurrection set Jews free from personal sin and guilt, incorporated the Gentiles, and offered "justification" by faith rather than by the Torah.

Paul himself struggled under the grip of sin and guilt in his personal life (Rom. 7), and even though he was "under the law blameless" (Phil. 3:6) he was searching for something new in his life as a Jew. On the Damascus Road he finally found in Jesus Christ what he had been looking for: the possibility of forgiveness of sins and reconciliation to God apart from the Torah. In this powerful, life-changing experience, Paul's sense of God and of Christ had changed: he had been "converted" from Judaism to Christianity.

This centuries-old interpretation of Paul and his theology had a pervasive effect, not only on the popular understanding of Paul himself, but also on that of Christianity generally. In the last half-century or so, however, there has been a revolution in Pauline studies that has left Paul looking radically different. Issues such as Paul's attitude to the Torah and his understanding of righteousness and justification have played their part in the emergence of the "new look," but the overall picture has changed as well. At the popular level the "new look" on Paul remains widely unknown, and it is the purpose of this chapter to outline some of the key features of the new thinking and to summarize what the significant differences are. In order to do this, I shall discuss the work of three key contributors to the debate: Krister Stendahl, E. P. Sanders, and J. D. G. Dunn. These have all attempted to release Paul from the grip of later interpretation and to set him in the context of the Judaism of his day. At almost every point, the centuries-old interpretation of Paul and his theology has crumbled and a radically new picture has begun to take its place.

Krister Stendahl

Although the roots of the recent revolution in Pauline studies go back at least to the nineteenth century, it is the work of Krister Stendahl halfway through the twentieth century that marks the beginning of a serious change in the perception of Paul and his theology. In an article titled "The Apostle Paul and the Introspective Conscience of the West" (1963) and in a book called *Paul among Jews and Gentiles* (1976), Stendahl claimed that Paul had been misinterpreted and misunderstood for centuries by being read in the light of the theological concerns of the Reformation in the sixteenth century, especially those of Martin Luther, and of

St. Augustine in the fourth century. For Stendahl, whereas the concerns of Luther and Augustine were with individual and personal sin, guilt, justification, and salvation (the "introspective conscience"), Paul's primary concern was more practical: the relation between Jews and Gentiles who were trying to live together in Christian communities in Paul's own day. Paul's overall theological interest was not with the individual human quest for salvation and justification ("How do I get saved?") but with the practical concern of how those who are saved and justified by God will live together in Christ ("How do Jews and Gentiles relate to each other?"). Stendahl's aim was to scrape away the Lutheran theological interpretation that had obscured Paul over the centuries and allow him to speak for himself.

Stendahl's work was particularly noteworthy as he himself is a Lutheran Bishop. A number of other major modern commentators on Paul, including Rudolf Bultmann and Ernst Käsemann, have in fact been Lutherans and have helped perpetuate the Lutheran interpretation of Paul. For them Paul began from a position in which he acknowledged his own and others' sinfulness and then saw the need of faith in Jesus Christ to put things right. But Stendahl argued that Paul was not a tormented and disillusioned individualistic Jew, obsessed with his own personal guilt and sinfulness and searching for a new pathway to God before he encountered Christ, but rather the other way around: Paul was concerned with the practical question of how Jews and Gentiles would relate to each other in the Christ-based communities with which he dealt. Part of Paul's answer to this problem was that in Christ the Gentiles had been incorporated into the people of God, or as Paul says, "justified." Stendahl knew that Paul was concerned with human sin, but maintained that this was not chiefly the personal sin of the individual and that in any case this was not Paul's primary concern in the sense usually imagined. Romans 7, for example, so often cited as the heart of the Pauline view of sin, is not actually the main focus of that letter. In the centuries after Paul, Stendahl claimed, Paul's practical concern with Jews and

Gentiles in the context of his apostolate slipped from view and his letters were interpreted in radically different contexts such as that of the European Reformation.

One of Stendahl's key illustrations of how Paul has been misinterpreted over the centuries concerns the word *paidagogos* in Galatians 3. It is well known that Paul was confronted with the problem of the law and its place in God's purposes once he began his new life "in Christ." In response to problems relating to Judaism in the church in Galatia, Paul claims that "the law was our custodian (*paidagogos*) until Christ came . . ." (3:24). In an earlier chapter we have seen that the word *paidagogos* in Greek can be translated "nanny," "schoolteacher," or "custodian," but these translations have different meanings and nuances in English and there have been different understandings of this word. In the past, Galatians 3:24 has been translated "the law was a schoolteacher," giving the impression of a stentorian figure exacting a particular standard and inducing a sense of guilt and individual personal failure. This understanding enhances the sense of the law as a legalistic system in which individuals strive for perfection but fail. For Stendahl, *paidagogos* is better translated as "custodian" or "caretaker," with the sense that the law had a positive but temporary role of looking after people until Christ came. Paul's concern here is not to do with legalism, personal failure, shortcoming, guilt, and sin, says Stendahl. Rather, the law had the totally positive role of taking care of God's people until Christ came but has now been superseded in Christ, for Jew and Gentile alike.

Stendahl's interpretation of Galatians 3:24 is symptomatic of his overall perception of Paul's theology and points to many other features of the "new look." Stendahl drew attention to five crucial points in his non-Lutheran interpretation of Paul. First, Paul's dramatic Damascus experience (Acts 9, 22, and 26; cf. Gal. 1) should be seen as a "call" rather than a "conversion." Paul's experience was not a "conversion" from one religion to another, but a "call" to specific action in the style of the prophets of ancient Israel, for example Jeremiah and Isaiah. The experience was not a "conversion" resulting from a personal, individual change from one religion to another, but a radical change of direction within Judaism (which while certainly personal, was not individualistic and private) in which Paul became the "apostle to the Gentiles." In other words, the event is to be seen within the community context of Jew-Gentile relations.

Second, says Stendahl, Paul's main concern was "justification not forgiveness." In the old understanding of Paul, in the paradigm of the "introspective conscience," it was claimed that the individual, riddled with sin and guilt, needed personal forgiveness and that this was available in Christ. But Paul hardly ever uses the word forgiveness (Rom. 4:7; cf. Col. 1:14; Eph. 1:7). His concerns are not with sin from an anthropological or psychological perspective, but simply with God's justification or acceptance of his people, Jews and Gentiles together, in the purposes of God.

Third, Paul was concerned with "weakness not sin." Paul does speak of his own weakness (2 Cor. 4:7–12; 11:21–29; 13:4), but weakness (*astheneia*) is quite different from sin (*hamartia*). Paul sees the power of God in weakness, and this includes his "thorn in the flesh," his illness, his humility, and even the power of Satan (2 Cor. 12:7–10; Gal. 4:13; 1 Thess. 2:18). But although he is concerned with the place of sin in human relations with God, he is not concerned with his own personal sinfulness and guilt as such.

Fourth, Paul is concerned with "love rather than integrity." Stendahl claims that for Paul, love (e.g., 1 Cor. 13) is more important than individual integrity or rights. In 1 Corinthians 8 and 10, for example, where there is a question about eating food that had been sacrificed to idols, Paul's answer is not that people should do what they personally as individuals believe to be right, but that they should hold back, where necessary, for the sake of the community. Once again, the question of practical relations between Jews and Gentiles is to the fore rather than individual concerns.

Finally, Stendahl claimed that Paul's teaching was "unique not universal." It was unique or specific to actual practical occasions within the community of Jews and Gentiles, rather than providing universal principles concerning sin and guilt by which individuals could live their lives and get saved.

In a short time and space, Stendahl painted a new picture of Paul. He turned the glass of perception around and revealed that the "introspective conscience," the concern with personal sin and guilt and with individual salvation, in fact had more to do with sixteenth-century Europe and the church of Luther's day with its problems of works and merit in relation to salvation, than it had to do with Paul himself. Stendahl showed that Paul was not an agonized individual who was forever looking inwards and who had become obsessed with his own sin and salvation, but a practical theologian whose concern was with the communities of Jews and Gentiles around him who had experienced Christ and who were trying to live together and respond to practical problems. Stendahl had started to "de-Lutheranize" Paul and to put him back into his proper historical context.

E. P. Sanders and J. D. G. Dunn

The foundations laid by Stendahl have since been built upon by two prominent Pauline scholars: E. P. Sanders and J. D. G. Dunn. Sanders' contribution lies largely in his reconstruction of the Judaism of Paul's day and in his portrayal of Paul within it. J. D. G. Dunn has contributed to the "new perspective" by pushing Sanders's insights to their logical conclusions. Let us look at them in turn.

E.P. Sanders

E. P. Sanders' contribution to the "new look" on Paul is twofold. First of all he has looked closely at the Judaism into which Paul was born, grew up, and lived until his Damascus experience; second, he has interpreted Paul's experience of Christ within that context. Sanders's works on Paul are *Paul and Palestinian Judaism* (1978); *Paul, the Law, and the Jewish People* (1983); and the much shorter *Paul* (1991). Sanders's most important contribution is to show how the Judaism of Paul's day was very different from that which has subsequently been constructed by Christians from the letters of Paul. Particularly, from relevant texts of the period, Sanders showed that Judaism was not a legalistic religion that emphasized righteousness through works and personal salvation through individual merit. It was, rather, a religion of salvation based on the covenant between God and his people Israel. Even though there were many different strands within Judaism, the covenant was basic to them all. Sanders emphasized that the covenant was prior to the law; it gave rise to the law, rather than the law giving rise to the covenant. Sanders coined the term "covenantal nomism" to sum up this basic emphasis of the Judaisms of the period.

Another element in Sanders's portrayal of Judaism at the time of Paul concerns its understanding of eschatology, or beliefs about the events of the end of the age. Sanders drew attention to the fact that most Jews of the period believed that God would act decisively for his people at the end of the age as he had done already in the past in creation and in history. They believed that God would draw all Jews to Jerusalem to Mount Zion where the new age would be ushered in. An important aspect of this Jewish eschatological expectation that is often overlooked was that the Jews would bring non-Jews or Gentiles with them to Zion. The literature of the period, often known as the "intertestamental literature," is imbued with this concept and it can already be found in the older Hebrew prophetic literature (Is. 2:2f.; Mic. 4:1f.). The God who had acted decisively in forming a people in the beginning and establishing a covenant with them would act decisively at the end time in bringing Jews and Gentiles together.

Covenant and eschatology are the two key features of the Judaism that Sanders sees as marking Paul. As a Jew, Paul claimed to be "under the law blameless" (Phil. 3:6). He was not looking for another path toward God; he was not discontent with his Jewish faith; he was not searching for a new path to salvation. However, God showed him something new by revealing his Son to him and appointed him to be the "apostle to the Gentiles," that is, the one who was to implement the incorporation of the Gentiles into the purposes of God in the end-time. For Sanders, Paul would have seen the incorporation of the Gentiles into God's purposes as part of God's eschatological act and would have counted his experience as thoroughly in line with his Jewish background. Paul's experience "in Christ" was, of course, radically new in Sanders's view, and Sanders has often been criticized for saying that what was wrong with Judaism for Paul after his Damascus experience was simply that it was not Christianity. Even so, for Sanders Paul was not founding a new religion. On the contrary, he worked within his communities to bring about the reconciliation of Jew and Gentile within Judaism.

Furthermore, he was not concerned with the salvation of individual, frustrated, legalistic Jews. His concern was not with a "doctrine" of "justification by faith" as contrasted with "works," but with the practical community concern of real Jews and Gentiles being incorporated into God's purposes. Sanders's understanding of Paul's teaching on righteousness and justification is that it is not "imputed" or simply given by God in Christ, but must be responded to in faith and is part of Paul's wider notion of a completely "new creation in Christ." In this context "justification" is a metaphor for "participation" in the new creation that Christ has established. For Sanders, Paul is the "apostle to the Gentiles," not because God's purposes with the Jews have become frustrated and hopeless, but because it is part of God's eschatological intention from the beginning that he will incorporate the Gentiles into his purposes. Paul is God's agent in bringing that final purpose about.

Overall, Sanders follows Stendahl in "de-Lutheranizing" Paul and putting him back into his first-century Jewish context. He then inverts the old picture of Paul and his significance as follows: instead of seeing Judaism as legalistic and Christianity as a religion of grace and forgiveness in which people can be "justified" by their faith, Sanders sees Judaism as a religion of salvation in which

God's purposes have been to incorporate the Gentiles all along. Paul is then seen as the eschatological "apostle to the Gentiles" whose main concern is with the relations between Jews and Gentiles in the wider purposes of God. In that context, Paul uses the language of justification as a metaphor for the new life that Jews and Gentiles can find in Christ when they respond in faith and practice. Even though Sanders's work has been at the center of the revolution in our understanding of Paul, it has not gone without criticism. In fact, J. D. G. Dunn has claimed that Sanders has not taken his own insights far enough.

J.D.G. Dunn

J. D. G. Dunn stands well within the school of Stendahl and agrees with most of Sanders's work, although he maintains that they could have taken matters further. Dunn's key works on this subject are an article titled "The New Perspective on Paul" (1982); a commentary on *Romans* (1988); *Jesus, Paul and the Law* (1990); and *The Theology of Paul the Apostle* (1998). Like Stendahl and Sanders, Dunn wishes to see Paul "de-Lutheranized" and put back in his own first-century Jewish context. For Dunn, Paul was not writing against Jews who were trying to earn their own salvation by legalistic self-seeking; nor was he writing against "good works" in a general moral sense. Rather, he was dealing with how Jews and Gentiles were to be incorporated into the purposes of God. Sanders claimed that Paul's Damascus experience brought something so radically new into Paul's existence that it ended up being something other than Judaism. By contrast, Dunn emphasizes Paul's continuity with Judaism even after his dramatic life-changing encounter with Christ.

Dunn's approach is to look at the details of Sanders's claim that Paul must be seen from within the Judaism of his day and to push these to their logical conclusions. Dunn's argument inevitably concerns the law and justification. For Dunn, when Paul is complaining about "works of the law" he means specific works of the law and not the law per se or "good works." In particular, he means circumcision, food laws, and festivals, especially the Sabbath. These things were the practices that gave the Jews their specific identity in Paul's time and bound them together nationally and racially. They were the national markers or badges of Jewish identity. Paul's argument in Romans and Galatians is then oriented against the nationalistic keeping of *specific* laws and expecting to gain God's favor by doing so. Paul's aim is to show such people that what had happened in Christ was also for the Gentiles. For Dunn, Paul's case is not against the law per se or against "good works" per se but against those who think they can gain God's favor by keeping certain laws, and who boast because they are Jews and think that they have particular privileges on those grounds. Dunn notes that "justification," "faith," and "being justified through faith" are already elements within ancient Judaism. Jews would have agreed with Paul that justification is by faith; both justification and faith were thoroughly central to Judaism.

What Paul is attacking is the "covenantal nomism" identified by Sanders: the notion that God's covenant with the Jews made them favored by God. Dunn claims that Sanders never explained satisfactorily why Paul moved away from Judaism to his own religion "in Christ." For Dunn, Paul didn't; he stayed within Judaism, seeing justification through Christ as continuous with justification under the law. In this case the law and Christ are not antithetical. Christ is the fulfillment of the law, and the two are continuous and complementary. For Dunn, Paul's experience in Christ remains more clearly an event within Judaism than it does for Sanders.

There has been a revolution in Pauline studies. The "new look" on Paul has provided a radically new picture of the "apostle to the Gentiles" and his theology. Since the old picture of Paul was often equated with Christianity itself, it is important that the new picture becomes as widely known as possible. The old picture was that Paul opposed a Judaism based on works-righteousness, a legalistic religion in which Jews tried to earn their own salvation by keeping the law as impeccably as they could. Paul's message, on this view, was that God had sent his son Jesus Christ to abolish all that and to establish a religion of grace and forgiveness. Indeed Christ had now "justified" sinners through their faith. This was basically a Lutheran interpretation. Luther's concern was with the personal salvation and justification of the individual and was opposed to the legalistic dimension of medieval Catholicism. By contrast, the "new look" shows that Paul was concerned more with the practicalities of Jewish and Gentile Christians living together in his communities. Stendahl "de-Lutheranized" Paul; Sanders put him back into his first-century Jewish context and emphasized that Judaism was a religion of salvation in which Paul was the "apostle to the Gentiles" appointed by God to usher in the last days; Dunn went further still and emphasized that Paul's experience left him well within the boundaries of Judaism itself. Far from moving from Judaism to something radically different in Christ, Paul remained Jewish to the end, albeit now "in Christ" who had fulfilled the law.

There have, of course, been many criticisms of the "new look" on Paul, including the notion that those who have established it and followed it have concentrated more on history than theology. But in any case, all those who would now paint a portrait of Paul and his theology must engage with the "new look" and with a Paul whose identity will be found primarily in his own historical context rather than that of Martin Luther.

NINE

PAUL AND CHRIST
CHRISTOLOGY, ETHICS,
AND ECCLESIOLOGY

I n modern western theology, christology, ethics, and ecclesiology
are usually dealt with as separate subjects, each receiving the spe-
cialized attention of highly skilled practitioners in the different
fields. Since the beginning of the Enlightenment period in Europe
these subjects have gradually developed their own methodological
approaches and concerns and have operated independently. It is rare
today, for example, to find a scholar working in christology or ecclesiology that links that study with a concern for contemporary ethical issues. Equally unusual is a Christian ethicist who focuses
specifically on the relation between ethics and the nature of the Person of Christ. But in actual Christian life and experience such sep-
arations can quickly seem inadequate. Beliefs about Christ interact
with Christian behavior and the formation of communities in his
name. Indeed, from the earliest days of Christianity, perceptions of
the nature of Christ have influenced notions of how those who
believe in him should actually live, worship, and think of the church.

St. Paul knew very well that christology, ethics, worship, and
ecclesiology are all fundamentally related, although this is not
always appreciated by modern readers of his letters. A close study
of two well-known Pauline passages and their contexts in the letters in which they occur helps show how interrelated these areas

really are for Paul and how theology and Christian life interact at the level of experience and worship. In this chapter, I offer detailed exegeses of the so-called christological hymns in Philippians 2:6–11 and Colossians 1:15–20. In the Philippians exegesis I show how Paul relates his christology to his ethics and the community life of the people to whom he is writing. In the Colossians exegesis I show how Paul relates ecclesiology, especially his notion of Christ as head of the church, to his christology.

Philippians 2:6–11

Philippians 2:6–11 comprises one of the great "christological hymns" of the New Testament. It is best known as the basis of "kenotic christology," that is, the theory that in the incarnation Christ "emptied himself" of his divine attributes. The interest in this essay is in the claims made about Christ and in the overall ethical setting of the passage. Paul's main concern in including this passage in his letter to the Philippians is to exhort them to be "of the same mind" (2:2). Much of chapter 1 and the first five verses of chapter 2 encourage the Philippians not to be selfish but to live together in love, showing concern for others. In 1:27 Paul begins to speak of the importance of the connection between the Philippians' way of life and the Gospel of Christ.

Although the content of Philippians 2:6–11 is christological, its wider setting within the letter is ethical. In fact, in Philippians, we have a model case of how ethics and christology are fundamentally related for Paul. It is not only that Christians must do what Christ did, in humility, following his example as some sort of ethical model. It is rather that the ethical requirements arise naturally out of Christ's involvement with creation. In approaching the claims that Paul makes about Christ in this passage, it is worth making some general observations about its background and literary structure.

The letter to the Philippians is one of Paul's so-called "letters from prison" written in the late 50s or early 60s of the first century CE. It is unclear, however, where Paul was in prison. According to Acts 16 he visited Philippi on his second missionary journey. Paul's concern in this letter is to exhort the recipients to stand firm in their faith in the face of opposition. The "christological hymn" of 2:6–11 may originally have been a pre-Christian hymn to which Paul has made Christian additions. It has a poetic, hymnic structure and it is likely that it also functioned as a hymn in early Christian worship.

There have been two main views of the structure of the hymn: the first, associated with Ernst Lohmeyer, claims that the passage divides into two sections, the two halves corresponding to a basic "descent-ascent" christological pattern as follows: (1) pre-existence (vv. 6–7); and (2) exaltation (vv. 8–11). The incarnation and death of Jesus then lie at the center of the two sections. The second view, associated with Joachim Jeremias, divides the passage into three sections, as follows: (1) pre-existence (vv. 6–7a); (2) earthly Christ (vv. 7b-8); and (3) exalted Christ (vv. 9–11). Here, the whole of Christ's incarnate life forms the central pin between the other dimensions of his existence. In both views the crux is Christ's humility and death and is reminiscent of Paul's views elsewhere (2 Cor. 5:21; 8:9; Eph. 4:9; cf. Heb. 2:6–9).

So what are Paul's actual claims in this passage? He introduces the christological hymn in 2:5 with an ethical exhortation: "Have this mind among yourselves, which you have in Christ Jesus." The connection between ethics and christology is already clear. Then, the first thing we learn about Christ is that "though he was in the form of God, (he) did not count equality with God a thing to be grasped" (v. 6). Christ's being in the "form of God" is an extremely difficult phrase to interpret. The words "form of God" are a translation of the Greek *morphe theou*. The word *morphe* is adequately translated as "form," but it is also closely related to the Greek *eikon* or "icon," meaning "image." What relation between Christ and God is Paul thinking of here? The connection of "form" with "image" may indicate a connection with Genesis 1:26 and Adam's creation in the image of

God. Most commentators have emphasized an "Adamic christol-ogy" here, which connects Christ with Adam, and it is clear that Christ is at the very least closely associated with God and is even in God's image. The main problem, however, is whether Paul intends more than that. Are we to see equality and identity between Christ and God implied in the word "form," as com-mentators traditionally have? Or is it that Christ is simply in the image of God, an image that all God's creatures share anyway?

The Greek word usually translated "though he was in" or "being" (i.e., in the form of God) is *huparchon*. This might mean "being" or "subsisting" and can imply "coming into existence" as much as "beginning." It is unclear, therefore, whether we are to think of this as implying a notion of the pre-existence of Christ when he is in the "form of God" or not. Traditionally, this verse, and the whole passage, has been thought to contain a notion of "pre-existence" similar to that found in John 1:1. However, it must be admitted that it is not logically necessitated by the actual words used in Philippians 2:6. Adam, who is in God's image in Genesis 1, is not thought thereby to be pre-existent, and maybe Christ isn't either. Whatever Paul intends, he obviously sees Christ as fundamentally very closely related to God.

When we turn to the remainder of verse 6, further difficul-ties arise. The text says that Christ "did not count equality with God a thing to be grasped." Not grasping at equality with God (*isa theou*) could suggest that Christ did not have equality with God in the first place. This would bear back upon what was meant by *morphe theou*. The Greek word for "grasping," *harpagmon*, is an extremely rare word and is again difficult to translate. It does not occur anywhere else in the New Testament; it is rare in Greek writing generally; and it is not in the Septuagint. In addition to this, and perhaps because of it, the meaning is ambiguous. Com-ing from the verb *harpazo*, it might mean "trying to grasp at some-thing not possessed at the time" (*res rapienda*) or being tempted in that direction. However, it can also mean trying to cling onto something actually already possessed (*res rapta*).

The question of which meaning is in Paul's mind here is difficult to answer. There are basically three alternatives: (1) Christ already had equality with God and might have held onto it, but he let it go; (2) Christ did not actually possess equality with God and, although he might have grasped after it, he did not do so; and (3) (a middle position) Christ did not exploit the relationship which he had with God. Rather, he renounced it and chose the path of humility and obedience, to be rewarded in the end by "super-exaltation."

The next words have been at the heart of kenotic christology. Paul says that Christ "emptied himself, taking the form of a servant." The statement that he "emptied himself" (*heauton ekenosen*) immediately begs the question, "Of what did he empty himself?" which bears back on what relation we reckon him to have had with God in the first place, that is, on what is meant by *morphe theou* and by *harpagmon* in verse 6. Are we then to think of Christ as pre-existent and as emptying himself of divine qualities in the incarnation, or as in the image of God and as emptying himself of that? Either way, Christ now takes up the "form of a slave" (*morphe doulou labon*) and comes in the "likeness and form of men."

Here the language of the slave (*doulou*) might suggest that the "suffering servant" passages of Isaiah lie behind the christology. However, the Greek word used here, *doulos*, is not the word used in the Septuagint for the suffering servant. The word in the Septuagint is nearly always *pais*, although *doulos* is used in Isaiah 49 in a general way for obedient servants of God. In any case, the idea that the "servant songs" constitute a group of texts with something in common that might influence later writers, dates only to the nineteenth century. We cannot be sure, therefore, that the "suffering servant of Isaiah" does lie behind Paul's concept of Christ here in Philippians.

We are further told that Christ comes in the likeness (*homoiomati*) of men, a position clearly contrasted with his previous condition. In verse 8 we come to the key point in the first half of the passage: "And being found in human form he humbled himself and became obedient unto death, even death on a cross." Here Christ is in the "form of man" or "human form" (this time *schemati* for "form"). Whatever understanding of "form of god" (v. 6) we take, whether that of pre-existence or that of Adamic "image," the hymn now reaches its halfway point in the death of Jesus on the cross. This is the point of ultimate humility and death, which is the basis for the subsequent "super-exaltation."

The second half of the passage does not raise quite so many exegetical problems as the first half. "Therefore God has highly exalted him and bestowed on him the name which is above every name . . ." (v. 9). The concern of the second half of the passage is with Jesus' super-exaltation (*huperupsosen*), seemingly to a higher status than he had before (cf. Ps. 8:6; 110:1). Once again, the interpretation of this will depend upon what position he had with God in verse 6. The "name which is above every name" (v. 10) here is, of course, "Jesus" (*Iesous*). He is also ultimately "Lord" (*kurios*, verse 11). The name of someone was significant in Hebrew and Greek language and culture, and summed up the personality, character, and significance of the person. "Jesus" is "savior" and ultimately "Lord." In the Septuagint the name of God is given as *kurios*, and wherever it is used of Jesus it could imply that he has the name of God. However, more generally the word *kurios* meant "sir" and was simply a polite form of respect. Here in Philippians it is possible that the name implies that Christ performs the work of God in his humility and death.

The final verses of the passage turn to a climax in which praise and worship dominate: "that at the name of Jesus every knee should bow, in heaven and on earth and under the earth, and every tongue confess that Jesus Christ is Lord" (vv. 10–11). In these verses the liturgical impact of the passage can easily be felt. Tongues confess and knees bend (*gonu kamphe*) in worship, and Jesus is confessed as Lord. It must be noted that the ultimate thrust of Philippians 2:6–11 is not only christological, but also thoroughly theological. All of this, the humiliation and the super-exaltation included, is not for Christ's own glory, but ultimately "to the glory of God the Father" (v. 11).

However we interpret the detail of Philippians 2:6–11, there are a number of key elements that are bound together in the passage and in the context: the christology is set in a context of ethical exhortation, and the hymn most likely had its original setting in the context of Christian worship.

Colossians 1:15–20

When we turn to Colossians 1:15–20 there are many similarities with Philippians 2:6–11, although the climate is rather different. This time, christology is bound up with ecclesiology and with creation itself. Some commentators have questioned whether Colossians is in fact by Paul, but many accept that it is and I shall follow them here. Very little is known for certain about the background to Colossians, but it is another "letter from prison" and was probably written in the 50s of the first century CE. There are a number of things about this passage that run parallel with Philippians 2:6–11: it is normally thought of as one of the great "christological hymns" of the New Testament; it seems likely that Paul took over a pre-Christian hymn and added to it; and it very probably originally had a setting in worship, both as a pre-Christian hymn and as a Pauline hymn. The situation to which Paul was writing in Colossae has been assessed in a variety of different ways, but it is clear that he was writing to correct what he considered to be false teaching of some sort. Whether this was some form of mysticism or gnosticism or a form of heterodox Judaism we cannot finally determine. Whatever the problem was, Paul was writing to reaffirm the full significance of Christ and to exhort the Colossians to maturity and stability in the real knowledge of God and of Christ (e.g., 1:10, 23, 28; 2:2; 4:12).

As with Philippians, the literary, poetic structure of Colossians 1:15–20 is important. There are basically two sections: (1) verses 15–18a; and (2) verses 18b–20. The first focuses on creation, the second on salvation. We will consider them in turn. The previous verses of the letter are about redemption and the forgiveness of sins through God's "beloved son" (v. 14). The hymn then opens with "He is the image (*eikon*) of the invisible God, the first-born of all creation" (v. 15). As with the Philippians hymn the language immediately suggests Adam's creation in the image of God in Genesis 1:26. The second part of the verse, however, suggests that wisdom might be the background here rather than Adam. Christ is "the first-born of all creation" (*prototokos pases ktiseos*) and like wisdom, he is the pre-existent instrument of creation. The close association of Christ and creation is clearly central here, and it is worth pausing to look briefly at what wisdom language might have meant to the Christians in Colossae in Paul's time.

Wisdom was an important concept in ancient Israel, and it was taken over by early Christians when they spoke about Christ. The notion of Jesus Christ as "divine wisdom," of course, was to become very significant later in Christian theology. The "wisdom" literature of Judaism is normally thought to be predominantly the books of Proverbs, Job, Ecclesiastes, Ecclesiasticus, and the Wisdom of Solomon. The Hebrew word *hokmah* is the word normally translated as "wisdom," and it has a broad range of meanings. It consists, first of all, of sayings or aphorisms that have arisen out of daily life and sum up the wisdom of practical living. These are then thought of as God's wisdom and personified in the literature as a beautiful woman. In Proverbs 8, for example, wisdom is a personified figure who calls out her message of wisdom to Israel. More importantly still, she is perceived as a dimension of God's nature. She is "the first of his acts of old" (v. 22). Proverbs 8 goes on to identify wisdom as being there at the beginning when God created the world; she is a part of God and of his work in creation; she is his instrument of creation; and she is a gift from God to those who will receive her (Prov. 2:6). She permeates and upholds creation.

There are different views as to whether wisdom was thought of as a separate part of God in some way during this period, or whether she is simply a literary personification. But it is not surprising that early Christians took up wisdom language in their worship and in their thinking about Christ. The logos concept used in the Prologue to the Fourth Gospel is closely associated with wisdom, or *sophia* in Greek, often said to be the feminine equivalent of the masculine *logos*. Colossians 1:15–20, then, draws on the Hebrew wisdom tradition in affirming that Christ is the "first-born of all creation." The main question here is whether Christ is to be thought of as one of God's creatures (the first-born in time) or as "first-born" before time and therefore pre-existent. This problem became central later in the controversy known as Arianism in the fourth century. In any case, in Colossians, Paul is clearly using a "wisdom christology."

The Colossians passage continues, "for in him all things were created, in heaven and on earth, visible and invisible, whether thrones or dominions or principalities or authorities—all things were created through him and for him . . ." (v. 16). Here, Christ is fundamentally associated with creation, and the christology is cosmic. Christ is associated with the various dimensions of creation and like wisdom he is seen as God's instrument of creation. But the language here also suggests that the creation is inherent in Christ. Various elements within creation, its hierarchical layers, are then listed. Both angelic powers (thrones and dominions) and worldly powers (principalities and authorities) are named in the hierarchical system of creation (cf. Rom. 8:38; 1 Cor. 15:24).

More important: "all things were created through him and for him." Here, the notion that Jesus Christ is the instrument of creation recalls John 1:3 and Hebrews 1:2f. The "through" and "for" are important: Christ is not only the instrument of creation; the creation is also "for him" and belongs to him. Then, "he is before all things, and in him all things hold together." Once again the wisdom influence is clear: Christ is pre-existent and like wisdom permeates creation, holding everything together in order. The next verse has often especially been thought to be a Pauline addition to the pre-Christian hymn because it mentions the church. The claim is that Christ is the "head of the body, the church" (v. 18; cf. 1 Cor. 12; Rom. 12). Here creation, christology, and ecclesiology can now all be seen to be fundamentally related. In Colossians the body image for the church is now used in the cosmic sense of the universal church rather than of the local church and incorporates all dimensions of the universe that have been named in previous verses. The church of which Christ is the head is itself related fundamentally to creation. Christ, creation, and the church are all interrelated here, and the church flourishes as part of the fullness of creation.

The position of Christ is then clarified further: "He is the beginning, the first-born from the dead, that in everything he might be pre-eminent" (v. 18). Wisdom language is again evident in "beginning" and "first-born" (*arche* and *prototokos*). Now, Christ is first-born "from the dead" and the resurrection is central to the christology and the ecclesiology. "For in him all the fullness of God was pleased to dwell" (v. 19). The word "fullness" (*pleroma*) here has received a great deal of comment and certainly became important in later Gnostic circles. Its meaning here is probably simply "all the things of God" as outlined in the previous verses, the angelic powers, including the dominions and principalities. It is "pleased to dwell" in the sense that it is God's will to dwell in Jesus.

Now the purpose or effect of that dwelling is named: "and through him to reconcile to himself all things" (v. 20). Reconciliation (*apokatallaxia*) is a key Pauline concept (2 Cor. 5:17–21) and the "all things" (*ta panta*) once again means "all creation," as is underlined by "whether on earth or in heaven." The reconciliation of all creation to Christ is brought about primarily through Christ's sacrificial death on the cross (cf. Rom. 3:25). This reconciliation inevitably brings about peace (cf. Rom. 5:1).

Overall, the passage sees Christ as the wisdom of God, the one in whom the whole creation holds together. But Paul also sees the church as part of creation and Christ. Everything is reconciled in Christ's death and resurrection. In this we find the deep roots of the connection between Christ, creation, and the church in Paul's thinking. And this passage, like Philippians 2:6–11, was probably originally used in Christian worship.

Modern western theology has separated its individual disciplines to an incredible degree over the last few hundred years. But Paul knew that for Christians, matters such as creation, Christ, ethics, ecclesiology, and worship are all fundamentally related and form parts of a single whole. It is clear from an exegesis of these two great "christological hymns" of the New Testament, Philippians 2:6–11 and Colossians 1:15–20, that Paul saw Christian life and behavior as integrally associated with the very nature of Christ himself. In both passages he alerts his readers to some basic connections: in Philippians, he sees underlying theological connections between the nature of Christ and the nature of Christian life. Christians are to behave in a manner continuous with Christ's behavior for them, i.e., "taking the form of a servant." Christ is not merely a moral example; his humility and death lead naturally to Christian humility in the community.

In Colossians, Paul uses wisdom language to underline Christ's place in relation to creation. Christ is the instrument of creation; he permeates it and upholds it. Then, in referring to many aspects of creation and using the body image, he shows how the church—of which Christ is head—is related to creation itself. Christ is the head of a church whose body has its place within the fullness of creation.

Here, christology and ecclesiology come together; ecclesiology is rooted christologically in Paul's notion of the church as those who are brought together and redeemed in the context of creation.

Finally, both passages were probably used in the context of early Christian worship, and Philippians comes to a dramatic end on a note of worship. Overall, both passages indicate that for Paul ethics, creation, ecclesiology, and worship are linked up with the very nature of Christ himself and that there can be no separation of these elements in Christian life or theology.

TEN

THE FALL AND ORIGINAL SIN
THE REAL MEANING
OF ROMANS 5:12–21

The popular Western Christian understanding of the Fall of Adam and of Original Sin does not come directly and simply from chapter 5 of St. Paul's epistle to the Romans and the book of Genesis chapters 1–3. It stems, rather, from the interpretation of those texts by St. Augustine in the fourth century and Martin Luther in the sixteenth. The idea that Adam and Eve were created by God as perfect creatures with free will who then misused that free will and "fell" from perfection, and that God then sent his son Jesus Christ to redeem the world from sin, is firmly fixed in the Western Christian psyche not only as the main view but as the only Christian view of "salvation history." More powerful still is the idea that all human beings somehow partake of Adam's sin itself; that his sin and our sin are directly causally related; that there is some sort of "seminal identity" between Adam and the rest of the human race down the ages; and that in Adam's sin we have all sinned. From the time of St. Augustine, this notion of "original sin" has formed the basis of the theology of infant baptism, and centuries of liturgy, theology, art, and music have seen "Adam's transgression" either as a disaster, or as a

113

"happy fault" that enabled salvation to occur in Christ. Not only is this view of the roles of Adam and Christ firmly fixed in the western imagination, it is also assumed that it is there for all to read in the pages of the Bible.

In fact, it can be found more clearly in Augustine and Luther than in Romans and Genesis. Down the centuries since Paul wrote Romans, layer upon layer of interpretation have obscured his words and his theology. In addition, there is at least one reading of Genesis that is somewhat different from the usual one (that of Irenaeus of Lyons in the second century CE) and that sees Adam and Eve in a completely different light from Augustine. In this chapter, I first discuss briefly some relevant issues on the Fall and Original Sin associated with Irenaeus, Augustine, and Luther; and second, I follow Paul's own argument in Romans 5:12–21 on Adam and Christ, paying close attention to Paul's Greek at crucial moments.

Irenaeus, Augustine, and Luther

Let us begin with the most familiar account of the Fall of Adam and of Original Sin as found in Augustine (CE 354–430), who did, of course, base much of what he had to say on this matter on the Genesis and Romans narratives. Augustine's theology on these matters was partly, though by no means wholly, a reaction to Pelagius, who maintained that human beings were capable of achieving salvation by their own efforts. By contrast, Augustine stressed the initiative of God in enabling humanity to leave its sin behind and embrace Christ. In his *Enchiridion*, written in the early 420s CE, Augustine says, "When Adam was created, he was of course righteous and a mediator was not needed. But when sin placed a wide gulf between mankind and God, a mediator was called for who was unique in being born, in living, and in being slain without sin, in order that we might be reconciled to God and brought by the resurrection of the flesh to eternal life. . . ." (xviii.108).

The idea that Adam was created in "original righteousness" or "original perfection" is the basis of the Augustinian view. Adam was created perfect and was given "free will," that is, the freedom to act as he wished. It is in this "free will" that Augustine locates the origins of sin and ultimately of all the evil and suffering that the human race brings about. In reading Genesis 1–3, Augustine marks the action of Adam and Eve in choosing to pick and eat the fruit of the tree of the knowledge of good and evil as the beginning of human sin. This so-called "transgression of Adam" not only alienated him and Eve from God, but also brought about a state of sinfulness in the human race, in which all human beings since Adam's time have participated. It is here that the heart of the doctrine of "original sin" can be pinpointed. Adam's transgression brought sin into the system, as it were, and human beings have been fundamentally separated from God ever since, apart, of course, from the redemption wrought in Jesus Christ. It is here, also, that the greatest difficulty lies, because Augustine bases this view on his Latin translation of Romans 5:12.

In most English translations today we read that "sin came into the world through one man" and then "because all men sinned." Augustine's Latin translation here, however, read "in whom all men sinned." We shall return to the language issues later, but for the moment it is sufficient to note that Augustine was using a translation of Paul's Greek that is less than satisfactory. For Augustine, once the sin and death in humanity has been associated with Adam, it takes on an organic connection with Adam's sin, and humanity becomes a *massa peccati* or *massa damnata*: a "mass of sin" or a "mass of damnation." Indeed, it is in Augustine that the expression *originale peccatum* (original sin) is first found.

It is in association with these expressions that Augustine also speaks of *originalis reatus* (original guilt) and of *concupiscentia* (concupiscence). Humanity since Adam is not only born in sinfulness, but also in guilt, and has a general tendency to sinfulness or concupiscence thereafter. Original sin is passed on at birth from parent to child, and there is a "seminal identity" or a causal relation between the sin of Adam and the sin of the rest of us. But God's image in humanity is not completely lost, and humanity is redeemable by Christ. Unlike Pelagius, Augustine stressed that although humanity is firmly in the grip of sin, God's grace in Christ enables salvation and the cleansing of sin.

In turning to the thought of Martin Luther (1483–1546), we find the same basic framework of thought that we have identified in Augustine on the Fall and Original Sin reiterated and developed. In many ways Luther represents a Reformation version of Augustinianism over a millennium later. For Luther, as for Augustine, Adam was created in original righteousness and perfection. Luther read Genesis as implying that Adam fell from this perfection and thereby delivered his sin to humanity down the centuries. Humanity, therefore, is thoroughly bound up with sin, has inherited sin, and stands in a state of sinfulness and guilt before God.

Luther also claimed that original sin was passed on through childbirth. He differs from Augustine in claiming that human beings are left with no free will after the fall and are totally in the grip of sin. Here Luther took the Augustinian line a step further and claimed that humanity is totally dependent upon the grace of God for redemption. Here he is at polar opposites to Pelagius and to his own earlier theology of the Fall. Luther's christology also develops vis-à-vis Augustine. In some of the most significant *christus victor* christology in Christian history, Luther claimed that Christ's death defeated sin and evil and restored the righteousness lost in the Fall.

We turn finally to the theology of Irenaeus of Lyons (CE 130–200) in order to show how the understanding of the Genesis narrative before Augustine was rather different from his and to show that Paul's understanding may have been different too. In the writings of Irenaeus, and in his reading of Genesis 1–3, there is no Fall as it is understood in Augustine and Luther. For Irenaeus, humanity was created innocent rather than perfect. That is to say, the human race was in a state of innocence like a child, rather than a state of human perfection or righteousness before God. Irenaeus used the Greek word *nepioi* (children) to indicate the state he thinks humanity was in at the beginning of creation. The development of the human race since the beginning of creation is then akin to a child growing up; there is development from the young to the old. Sin and evil are seen, not as the result of one dramatic "fall of Adam," but as "slips along the way" in the style of a child who makes mistakes. Irenaeus saw the fall of Adam in the Genesis narrative as one of the many slips or sins that human beings make along the road to perfection. Although human beings are made in the "image" of God, they are gradually growing toward the "likeness" (Gen. 1:26). In this reading of Genesis, human beings are like Adam in that everybody does sin, but they do not all participate in Adam's sin and certainly not in his guilt. In fact, this reading of the Genesis narrative is more congruous with what Paul himself seems to be saying in Romans 5:12, that all human beings have as a matter of fact sinned, because they are human, not because they are causally and organically related to Adam.

It is clear, then, that the notion of the Fall and of Original Sin as it has come to be known in the West can be found clearly in Augustine and Luther. But Augustine's theology of original sin was based on his Latin translation of the key texts, and Luther's readings were caught up in the polemics of the Reformation. Moreover, it is also clear that before Augustine's time, Irenaeus read Genesis in a different way and had a different theology of sin and redemption. To what extent, then, is any of this actually part of Paul's theology in Romans? Bearing in mind that Paul possibly read Genesis in a manner significantly different from Augustine, we shall now look closely at what he says about Adam in Romans 5:12–21.

Romans 5:12–21

In the first chapters of Romans, Paul draws attention to the fact that humanity is under the power of sin. Chapters 5–8 form a section relating to the possibility of new life in Christ. In 5:1–11, Paul writes of the justification and reconciliation brought about in Christ. Now, continuing the same interest, he writes in verses

12–21 specifically of what Christ has done for humanity in relation to sin. In Romans 4, Paul has used Abraham in order to illuminate the significance of Christ. Now in chapter 5 he uses
Adam. The key concern here is with Paul's teaching about Adam
and Christ, and about how each is related to humanity as a whole.

In 5:12 Paul writes of the sin that "came into the world
through one man." Paul is referring to Adam and the Genesis narrative whose key events he would have taken as historically true,
but he would not have known the Augustinian interpretation. The
familiar story of Adam and Eve eating the fruit of the tree of the
knowledge of good and evil occurs in Genesis 3. In Romans 5,
Paul writes that sin and death have spread to all men "because all
men sinned" (v. 12). There is no doubt that in Paul's mind Adam
has sinned and that sin and death are universal. However, the key
question here is exactly how Adam's sin is related to subsequent
sin, i.e., the sin of the rest of humanity.

We have already noted that the Latin translation used by
Augustine did not do justice to Paul's Greek. In fact, neither do
some English translations. In Romans 5:12, Paul writes *eph ho
pantes hemarton*. Augustine translated Paul's *eph ho* which meant
"in that" as *in quo*, which could mean either "in that" or "in
whom." Augustine interpreted Paul as meaning "in whom," and
this then influenced the whole Western tradition of interpreting
this verse. Let us look more closely at this problem.

Paul's words have been translated into English in two very different ways: first, as meaning "in whom" all sinned. This expression
does translate the Latin *in quo* that Augustine used. Augustine knew
little Greek and would have known this translation from some
commentaries on Paul's epistles by the unknown author usually
known as Ambrosiaster and formerly but wrongly thought to be
Ambrose. The translation "in whom" is a correct translation of the
Latin here, but the question is whether the Latin is a correct translation of Paul's Greek, which is *eph ho*. The translation "in whom"
does indeed give the impression that humanity has sinned "in
Adam" and that there is a direct causal connection between Adam's

sin and that of subsequent generations. This connection would indeed be the "seminal identity" that the later notions of original sin taught. The notion of "seminal identity" between Adam and the rest of humanity was certainly around in Paul's time and can be found in the nearly contemporary 4 Ezra 3:7–12. But this does not, of course, mean that it must be in Romans 5 or that "in whom" is the correct translation of Paul's *eph ho*.

The second possible translation of Paul's Greek words is "because," "in as much as," or "in that." This is, in fact, the most common English translation today, even though many people still assume the meaning "in whom"! In the second possible translation the fundamental relation between Adam and subsequent generations is different. "Because" is possibly ambiguous, but "in as much as" and "in that" simply note parallel states of affairs. Later sins are in line with Adam's sin but not directly caused by it. That is to say that it is part and parcel of human nature to sin, and sin and death have spread after Adam "in as much as" all people have sinned. The translation "because" should be understood here in the same way. Sin and death have spread "in as much as" or "in that" all people sinned. That is, all people have this sinfulness in common with Adam. It can be seen that the second translation is much less specific, lacks any causal connection between Adam and subsequent generations, and lacks any notion of "seminal identity" between Adam and his successors. It is simply the case that everybody sins.

The presence of Adam here is significant in a number of ways. Paul's use of typology is very powerful, and Abraham has already been used in Romans 4. In that argument, Abraham is connected to those who have been justified apart from the Law because he existed before the Law was given. The connection here is one of a type: one figure is used to illuminate the place of Gentile believers who are justified apart from the Law. In Romans 5 the mechanism is somewhat different because we have a figure that is contrasted with Christ. In 5:14 Adam is referred to as the *tupos tou mellontos*, that is, the "type of the one to come." There has been a good deal of debate over whether Adam is really a "type" and over who is the "one to come" here. Adam is really to be contrasted with Christ and is not strictly speaking a "type," although Paul does use the word. Adam is rather an "anti-type" or analogy. Adam and Christ are then in analogous situations: one is obedient, the other is disobedient. The relationship is, therefore, one of contrast. But the relation between Abraham and Gentile believers is much like that between Adam and sinners: they are in similar situations. It certainly seems clear that Christ is the "one who is to come" here, although some have suggested that it might be Moses.

A further matter relating to Adam is worth consideration. This is the notion of a primordial or primal man figure. The idea that an ideal figure typified the human race can be found in many of the cultures of the ancient world. This *Urmensch* or "first man" tradition has been traced to cultures such as India and Persia, and has been identified in Jewish, Christian, and Islamic texts. Such a figure was not only associated with the beginning of time but was also strongly associated with the end of time and was, therefore, an eschatological figure summing up the beginning and the end. It is possible that such a figure was also popular in Gnostic circles. If Paul is drawing upon any or all of these traditions, then his use of the Adam figure has immense significance christologically, for Christ is an extension of Adam. In 1 Corinthians 15 he is the last Adam and the second Adam (vv. 22ff., 45, 47). Overall, however, the point here is that the *Urmensch* figure represents and typifies humanity, but doesn't stand in a causal relation to it.

We must now turn to the other material in the passage in order to fill out the wider picture. Paul mentions the place of the law in relation to sin. Apart from the law sin is not counted. But sin is still powerful where there is no law. Verse 15 then turns to the role of Christ, with whom Adam has been contrasted. Another brief reference to Adam's trespass leads onto Paul speaking of the "free gift of grace" which comes in Christ. Grace is the free gift of God, and here is that which overbalances the sin of Adam. This is now offered "for many" (*hoi polloi*), which means "for everybody." It has the sense of "universal" and is available for all. It is not "many as opposed to all," but means the whole tribe, class, or clan, in this case "the human race."

The metaphor of justification, so powerful in Romans 1–8 and Galatians 3–4, is now introduced. The language of righteousness needs to be interpreted in terms of the possibility of a relationship and not in terms of the imputing of a character. So, likewise, the language of Adam's sin and trespass should be understood in terms of relationship and not of character. The free gift of God's grace (*charis*) brings the possibility of justification or righteousness. In verse 17 we are told that the relation between sin and grace is not equal. Again in verse 17 we have "because of one man's trespass death reigned through that one man." Here the Greek words *ei gar to henos paraptomati ho thanatos ebasileusen dia tou henos* are ambiguous, and do not have to imply seminal identity. Death has come "through" one man. Adam has certainly been the first, and has introduced sin and death, but we need not see here a causal relation between him and all men. It is still a matter of a new relationship being set up, and subsequent generations sinning through the relationship having been set up in Adam. In verse 17, as before, it is no more the case that human beings all necessarily sinned after Adam's sin, than it is that all human beings necessarily do righteous acts after being "made righteous" in Christ. They clearly do not, in either case.

One might easily object that verses 18 and 19 affirm a more direct "seminal identity." Paul writes of the contrast between what has happened in Adam and what has happened in Christ. In English, the translations are: "as one man's trespass led to condemnation for all men . . ." (*eis pantas anthropous eis katakrima*) (v. 18) and "as by one man's disobedience many were made sinners" (*hosper gar dia tes parakoes tou henos anthropou hamartoloi katestathesan oi polloi*) (v. 19). The crucial Greek words behind "to" or "led to" (*eis*) and "were made" (*katestathesan*) are ambiguous but in any case do not necessitate a full-blown Augustinian doctrine of original sin and "seminal identity."

Paul's words here must be seen in the context of his overall theology of sin and justification. The new situation that has been established in Christ concerns the possibility of a new relationship rather than the imposition of a new character. In terms of justification, this does not mean being "made righteous," but being given the possibility of becoming righteous through response in faith. In the same way, being "made sinners" does not mean simply being a sinner because Adam was. It means rather, being in a sinful condition in the same way that Adam was. In other words, sin is no more imputed in Adam than righteousness is in Christ. These verses must, therefore, be understood in terms of the relationship between humanity and God typified in Adam. Adam is a typical human being and is in that sense representative of humanity and its tendencies. Romans 5:20–21 then reasserts what has been said all along: that the law increased the trespass (through making people aware of sin); but grace outweighs the trespass; sin is related to death; grace is related to righteousness. All this culminates in "eternal life" (*zoen aionion*) and is brought about "through Jesus Christ our Lord."

It thus seems that at the very best the later notions of the Fall and Original Sin are developments of Paul's words. At the worst, they are a betrayal. The later, fully-fledged notion of the Fall and Original Sin has entered in through Western Latin translations and interpretations of Paul and is not part of his original understanding of the matter.

We must tread carefully in translating Paul's Greek in Romans 5, and in assuming what understanding of Adam he would have had. The notion that human beings were created perfect and given free will; that Adam and Eve "fell" from their perfection through eating of the fruit of the tree of the knowledge of good and evil; and that all human beings have subsequently been related to Adam in the sense of "seminal identity" and born in a condition of "original sin," are not to be found in Romans 5:12–21. Furthermore, the notion that Adam's "Fall" in Genesis 3 must be understood as an archetypal Fall affecting all humanity is far from clear in Romans 5. All of these notions have come from later readings of the text and largely from the Latin translations of Paul's own words. Augustine and Luther both developed the ideas of the Fall and Original Sin as they have come to be known in the West, but they are not to be found in Paul's Greek. In Romans 5 the emphasis is on the change in relationship between God and humanity that has been brought about in Adam and especially, of course, in Christ. Just as the notion of "imputed righteousness" is not in Romans, so the idea that in Adam human beings were "made sinful" in the sense of the later doctrines of Original Sin is not there either.

Adam is a figure who represents and typifies humanity as in the traditions of an *Urmensch* or primal man in the ancient world, but he is not seen by Paul as related seminally or organically to all subsequent generations. Even though there are major differences between Irenaeus and Paul, then, the real meaning of Paul's words in Romans 5:12–21 is closer to Irenaeus's theology than to that of Augustine and Luther: Adam typifies humanity in its sinfulness rather than causes humanity to sin.

ELEVEN

JUSTIFICATION BY FAITH?
PAUL'S THEOLOGY OF RIGHTEOUSNESS

Most Christians are familiar with the expression "justification by faith." At the popular level it is usually thought of as "justification by faith *alone*" and is associated with St. Paul and the alleged contrast he makes in his letters between faith and works. On the face of it, Paul seems to be claiming that it is faith rather than works that will justify sinners in the eyes of God, and that those who simply have faith will be justified or saved. However, it is not widely realized that Paul himself never uses the expression "justification by faith" or that his epistles have been read for centuries through the eyes of later theologians whose interests and concerns were other than his. The translation of Paul's epistles into Latin, their interpretation by St. Augustine in the fourth century, and their use by Martin Luther and others in the heat of Reformation polemics in Europe in the sixteenth century, have all left Paul's own mind buried in layers of later interpretation.

The popular understanding of Paul's theology of justification today owes more to later thinkers than to Paul himself. Two things are important here: first, that the medieval concern with good works and indulgences has clouded Paul's real concern with "works of the Law" in his own day; and second, Patristic and Reformation notions of God simply imputing righteousness to those who have faith, or making or declaring them righteous, is a long way from Paul's own notion of God offering the possibility of a new relationship with him to be responded to in faith. In New Testament Studies in the last couple of decades there has been a complete revolution in the understanding and interpretation of Paul on precisely this issue. The Patristic and Reformation interpretations of Paul have been scraped away to reveal a clearer though still complex theology of righteousness in Paul's letters.

So in this chapter, I first outline the background and meaning of the language of justification and righteousness as Paul received it from Judaism; second, I consider some of the problems of translation of Greek words used by Paul in his theology of justification; third, I outline the framework of thought in which Paul's notion of justification appears; and finally, I examine what Paul actually says about justification in his epistles to the Romans and the Galatians.

The Background in Judaism

Paul's theology of justification can be found in his letters to the Romans and the Galatians. In order to see clearly what he himself has to say about justification we must look at the words he actually uses. Behind the English words for justification and righteousness there lies a family of Greek words with the root *dik*. The word Paul uses mostly is *dikaiosune*, which is translated into English both as "justification" and as "righteousness." The Hebrew word that lies behind the Greek *dikaiosune* is *tsedek*, the basic root of which is simply *sdq* and means "to make straight," as in a rod or ruler. By implication *sdq* can also mean "to put right" or "to vindicate." It can also be translated as "righteousness." Thereafter, the range of meanings turns out to be quite broad. One of the main uses of *tsedek* in ancient Israelite society was in the law courts. Its meaning there was not only legal but also ethical and was associated with "justice."

The word occurs frequently in the Hebrew Bible and is translated into English in a number of different ways. It can refer to God's own nature and actions, for example in the Song of Deborah in Judges 5:11, which speaks of the "triumphs of the Lord." Here the Hebrew word *tsedekah*, the plural of *tsedek*, has been translated as "triumphs." The sense is one of God carrying out his just actions and becoming triumphant in war. In 1 Samuel 12:7 the translation of *tsedekah* is "saving deeds."

The translations "righteous" and "righteousness" are quite common: e.g., God's "righteous judgment" (Ps. 9:4); God will raise up a "righteous branch" (Jer. 23:5f.); "a king will reign in righteousness" (Is. 32:1); a righteous man and the way of righteousness (Ezek. 18:5–9 and 25–29); "everlasting righteousness" (Dan. 9:24); and "let justice roll down like waters, and righteousness like an everflowing stream" (Amos 5:24; cf. 5:7).

The word can also be translated as "justice": e.g., "justice for a light to the peoples" (Is. 51:4). The translation "vindication" is also found: e.g., God works "vindication and justice" (Ps. 103:6); "vindication . . . as brightness" (Is. 62:1); and the nations will see God's "vindication" (Is. 62:2). So, the Hebrew word *tsedek* can be translated as "triumphs," "saving deeds," "righteousness," "justice," and "vindication." It is associated with God's nature, justice, and right dealings with the world.

The language of righteousness and vindication was gradually taken into the law courts of ancient Israel and became a central forensic image. It is usually assumed that when someone was justified in that legal context the language had to do with acquittal in that the penalty for the crime was not paid. The criminal was not so much "made innocent" as "declared innocent" in spite of the crime. Are any of these senses indicative of Paul's use of the Greek word in his letters?

Translating Paul's Greek

Before turning to Paul's theology of justification in Romans and Galatians it will help to look closely at the problems that arise in trying to translate his Greek into English. We have already noted that in relation to his theology of justification, Paul uses a family of words with the root *dik*. His most frequent words are the noun *dikaiosune*, the verb *dikaioo*, and the adjective *dikaios*. The first thing to note is that whereas Paul uses one family of words with one root, one metaphor in fact, the English translations have two families of words to cover what he says: "justification" and "righteousness." Why is this? It is important to pursue this question not only as an interesting problem in translation of Paul's Greek, but also because caught up in the translation problem is the theological problem of what Paul was intending to say when he used his single family of words.

In fact, the problem of translation here focuses the difference between the Patristic and Reformation interpretations of Paul's theology of justification and what more clearly seems to be his own. Thus, when we begin to translate Paul's Greek, the problem emerges immediately. It is acceptable to translate the noun *dikaiosune*, like the Hebrew *tsedek*, as "righteousness." But when it comes to translating the corresponding verb *dikaioo* into English there is no verb that fits. Apart from the old English word "rightwise" which some have suggested here, there is only "to make righteous." The problem with this, as we shall see in the next section, is that it does not reflect what Paul says in Greek about what God is doing, that is, he is not "making people righteous." The words "to make righteous" carry the Patristic and Reformation theology of "imputation" and are an inadequate rendering of Paul's overall meaning.

Thus, English translators of Paul's texts turned instead to what the Latin translation of the Bible already had anyway, that is, "to justify" (Latin *justificatio; justificare*). Once the verb "to justify" has been used to translate the Greek *dikaioo*, a new noun appears: "justification." In the English translation of Paul's letters today, we therefore have two families of words, "justification" and "righteousness," where he has only one, *dikaiosune*. Even though some commentators maintain that there is a distinction in Paul's meaning in Greek reflected in the translations "justification" and "righteousness," this view is quite hard to sustain. At this point where language and theology are so thoroughly intertwined we must be very careful to try to see what Paul really intended. In struggling to speak of the new relationship between God and humanity brought about in Christ, Paul uses a legal metaphor from Judaism that means "making straight" and carries connotations of acquittal and forgiveness. What did he mean when he used this metaphor, and what are the key elements of his theology of justification and righteousness?

The Framework of Paul's Thought

Paul never tells us specifically what he means by justification and righteousness. As we have seen, it is a metaphor taken from the law courts of ancient Israel that he uses to speak about the new relationship God has set up between himself and humanity in Jesus Christ. In order to try to see what Paul meant, let us note first the general theological framework into which his justification language fits, and then outline briefly the place of the Jewish law in relation to justification.

It is perhaps confusing that Paul uses the language of justification and righteousness at the same time as using other metaphors for the new relationship in Christ. He also deals with other problems at the same time. Even so, it is clear that for Paul the death and resurrection of Jesus lie at the heart of the change in the relation between God and humanity. God has acted decisively in Jesus Christ to bring about the new relationship, and it focuses on Jesus' sacrificial death and on God raising him from the dead. This is coupled to a radical change in Paul's own awareness of God, of sin, of faith, and of the whole Jewish past. Whether we think of Paul's dramatic change of perception in terms of his Damascus Road experience as recounted in Acts (9, 22, and 26) or as a longer drawn-out experience such as he himself describes (Gal. 1), the fact remains that his entire perception of God and the things relating to God has now been refocused on Christ. This meant that, for Paul, the whole business of God's purposes in Israel, in the covenant, in the Torah as Paul had so far understood them had now changed and were seen through the lens of Christ.

This did not simply eliminate the past. Indeed, it is important to remember that, however we see Paul's dramatic experience, he did not see himself as parting from the purposes of God in Judaism. Rather, he saw himself as inhabiting the same religion, now in a new key. He saw his new life "in Christ" as "fulfilled Judaism"—for him, "Judaism as it should be," "Judaism in its right relation to God." The new relationship that had been inaugurated in the death and resurrection of Christ must be responded to in faith. But it must also be spoken of in terms of metaphors and images that Paul already knew from his own culture. In Christ, God had been active in reconciling the world to himself (2 Cor. 5:19) and had opened up the possibility of "making things straight" with humanity, or of vindicating or acquitting his alien-ated and sinful people. He had begun a process of "straightening out" the relationship and offering the possibility of a new begin-ning to be received in faith. The problem was, where did this now leave the past and God's purposes in Israel, covenant, and Torah? A brief look at the place of the Torah in Judaism, and now that God had acted in Christ, will throw Paul's notion of justification into sharper relief.

Israel, the covenant, and the Torah had been absolutely central to Paul's life and experience. When Paul mentions the Torah, he often means the covenant and Israel as well. They were central to practical living as well as to notions of what God was like. The Hebrew word *torah* has mostly been translated into English as "law," whereas "instruction," "guidance," and even "lore" are gen-erally thought to be better. The English word "law" gives the impression of an abstract system of rules imposed upon people by an external force or authority and which they must keep if they are to reap the full benefits of the system whose law it is. Of course, Torah did incorporate what is meant by the English "law," but it also meant much more. The word "lore" is particularly helpful as it retains the narrative aspect of the Torah and therefore its all-pervading power as a way of seeing the world. Since at least the time of the exile (c. 586–536 BCE) the Torah had been the lens through which Jews saw the world; it was their guide to living, and in Paul's day, it formed their entire understanding of what God had done for his people. It was not just a system of rules, but a symbol of the relationship that God had established at Sinai, of the Decalogue, and of the leading of the people into the land of Israel.

Paul took all this for granted, but everything had changed now that he had experienced Christ. Indeed, the change had been so radical that Paul could write in Romans that "Christ is the end of the Law" (10:4). Paul had come to see that righteousness had been made available to everyone "apart from law" (3:21) and claims that in Christ the whole structure of divine-human relations had changed, that human beings might be "justified" in a new way. That new way, however, did not mean that God had changed his mind or that the Torah had not been a thoroughly necessary and good part of God's purposes. Paul's attitude to the Torah in Romans and Galatians is complex and sometimes ambiguous. But it is worth pursuing what he says. The law has had a place in making people aware of sin, and even caused sin (Rom. 7:5, 7). It pointed forward to Christ (Rom. 4; Gal. 4); but in Christ people are delivered from the law (Gal. 3:2–5); it is no longer important for salvation (Rom. 3:30; 4:11; Gal. 6:15); Christ is the "end of the law," meaning its fulfillment (Rom. 10:4). However, the law is "holy and just and good" (Rom. 7:12), and was always necessary in God's purposes even though it is so no longer (Gal. 3:24). Indeed, Paul's overall point in all this is that even though the law was central in God's dealing with humanity, it is so no longer. For Paul, Christ had now become the vehicle of justification and righteousness. The new relationship had been established in Christ, and the metaphor of justification was used by Paul in order to try to articulate it.

Romans and Galatians

Paul's theology of righteousness and justification appears in Romans 1–8 and Galatians 3–4. It is probably better to focus on the letter to the Romans while keeping an eye on the shorter Galatians. The occasions for which the letters were written were different, as of course were their audiences, but the metaphor of justification functions in pretty much the same way in both letters.

The early chapters of Romans are concerned with human sinfulness before God. In Romans 1:16 Paul says that he is not ashamed of the Gospel and that it is for Jew and Gentile alike. The practical question of who is incorporated into the new relationship with God in Christ is clearly important and has even been claimed by some to be Paul's central concern. In relation to Jews and Greeks alike, Paul speaks of the "righteousness of God" (*dikaiosune theou*) in which the Gospel is rooted. Here, in the first occurrence of the word in Romans we see that the righteousness that has been made known in Christ is rooted in the righteousness of God himself.

The link with faith (*pistis*) is also made here in what is, however, a notoriously ambiguous quotation of Habakkuk 2:4. The ambiguity is already in the Greek of the quotation itself, and lies in the question of whether to translate the verse as "He who through faith is righteous shall live," or as "The righteous shall live by faith" (Rom. 1:17).

The considerable difference here takes us back again to the main problem of the relation between righteousness and faith. Are people righteous because they have faith? Or, are those who are righteous by other means supposed to live by the faith they have in response to that righteousness which God has given them? These options sum up the views that have been had of Paul's understanding of God's righteousness. Perpetrators of the recent revolution in Pauline studies have favored the second alternative.

The heart of Paul's notion of justification comes in Romans 3:21–26. Here, as we have already noted, he says that "the righteousness of God has been manifested apart from the law" (v. 21). This righteousness is "the righteousness of God through faith in Jesus Christ for all who believe" (v. 22). For Paul, the free gift of grace has been given through Jesus' death, and this makes righteousness available to all. Romans 3:25 lies at the heart of Paul's understanding of Jesus' sacrificial death. The important thing to note is that this is the means by which righteousness has been made available and by which those who respond in faith are "justified." Even though Paul uses the same basic word in 3:26 (*dikaioun* and *dikaiounta*), there are two levels to the process: the righteousness of God, and the process by which the believer becomes justified. Those who follow the most recent revolution in Pauline studies agree that Paul is speaking here of a new possibility, a new relationship that has been opened up by God in Christ. Those who respond in faith (*pistis*) or trust in God's initiative in Christ will enter into the new relationship. It is not a mechanical imputation that means human beings will automatically henceforth always do righteous acts. It is not that believers are automatically "made" righteous, but that they have a new possibility before them to which they may or may not respond in faith. Their response in faith will then, as it were, activate the process of justification.

In the subsequent chapters of Romans, Paul extends his basic understanding of what has happened. In Romans 4 (cf. Gal. 3) he introduces Abraham into the argument. Abraham is an ideal figure for Paul because he was not "justified by works" (of the law) (4:2). Paul quotes Genesis 15:6 (part of the law itself) in order to show that Abraham was righteous apart from the law. By this use of typology, Paul demonstrates that it is possible to be justified apart from the law (4:13). He now uses Abraham to support his claims that it is again possible to be justified apart from the law,

this time in Christ (4:24–25). In Romans 5 the argument introduces Adam, and the contrast between Adam and Christ also bears
on how justification is to be understood. In 5:19 Paul says, "For
as by one man's disobedience many were made sinners, so by one
man's obedience many will be made righteous." The English
translation here certainly gives the impression that the two
processes are simply ones in which sinners are "made" and righteous people are "made" respectively. However, the Greek gives no
such impression. It is not the case for Paul that people were only
able to do sinful acts because of Adam, and it is no more the case
that Paul thinks that people are only capable of doing righteous
acts because of Christ. It is rather, once again, a question of a new
relationship being established in which people are able to do
righteous acts through the response of faith. Some theologians in
the Reformation period spoke of God "declaring" sinners righteous. The business of being justified is then a process that continues this declaration. However one understands the words, it seems
that the real effectiveness of the process lies not just in God doing
everything, even though he takes the initiative, but in God and
humanity working together in the process. To be "justified" is to
accept the offer made by God in faith and to act accordingly.

What then is the real role of faith in all this? In Romans 9–11
Paul faces the broader question of the Gentiles and their part in
God's purposes vis-à-vis Israel. There have been many interpretations of these chapters and their relation to the rest of Romans,
but the key thing here is to note the place Paul gives to faith. The
Gentiles are now incorporated into the possibility of the new relationship through the death of Christ if they have faith. Like Abraham, they can be justified if they have faith. The famous allegory
of the olive tree (11:16–24) caps the whole argument here: it is
not a matter of whether one comes from the right stock, or has
circumcision and the law. Jews who have these things can be cut
out of the tree. Gentiles can be grafted in if they have faith. Like-

wise, unbelieving Gentiles can be chopped out and believing Jews grafted in again (11:23). The issue here, however, is not that they are admitted to the new relationship in Christ on the basis of their faith, but as we have learned in 3:25, the relationship is to be received in faith. Faith is the human side of the process. In Romans 9:30 Paul says that it is faith rather than works which are the issue, but Paul means works of the law here, or the law itself, rather than "good works." The "works" in Paul's arguments are simply "the law," which is no longer the location of the revelation of God's righteousness: it is now Christ. And in all this, faith is not the basis of justification and righteousness but a possible response to an offer made by God.

So what did Paul mean when he used the language of justification and righteousness? At the popular level, and down the centuries since Augustine and through the Reformation period, theologians and commentators on Paul have claimed that "justification by faith" is something primarily carried out by God on the grounds of faith alone. Partly in reaction to Pelagius, Augustine claimed that God "made" sinners righteous. Partly in reaction to his own earlier Pelagian tendencies Luther later claimed that it was God's action that is primary in the whole process of justification. This led to later Reformation views that were similar to Augustine's, that God had "made" sinners righteous.

Yet from this study of the words Paul actually uses and the context in which he uses them, we have seen that justification is primarily a law courts metaphor for a new relationship. In ancient Israel the word *tsedek* had a wide range of meanings, including the sense of acquittal, or of sinners being "declared" righteous. However, from Paul's own texts it is clear that although he uses a legal metaphor, he by no means intends a legalistic meaning. If we are to understand Paul to mean that sinners are "declared" righteous, they are certainly not automatically "made" righteous. In Romans 3:25f., those who are "justified" are those who respond in faith to the possibility of a new relationship that has been made available to them by God through the death of Christ. It is not a matter of merit, or of earning one's justification by having faith. Nor is it simply a matter of divine imputation, or making sinners righteous regardless of their behavior. It is the establishment of a new possibility that can be received through the response of faith. God works with humanity in the justification of his people, and they may or may not respond to him in faith. They are not simply "made" righteous but are given the opportunity of participating in a new relationship established by God in Christ.

EPILOGUE

Whether you have read *Paul Today: Challenging Readings of Acts and the Epistles* from cover to cover or have simply dipped into some chapters, I hope you have seen that important new things are happening in Pauline studies. It is an exciting and challenging area that is giving scholars new ideas of who Paul was and what he said. The implications of this for modern Christianity are enormous. No longer are we to think of Paul as a man who was simply against all the enjoyable things of life or who was negative about certain human relationships. No, a picture of a much more complex figure is emerging: one of Paul the struggling pastor who was trying as best he could to bring his new experience of the risen Christ to people in very different places and circumstances.

Although Paul was confident of his own faith in Jesus and his place in God's purposes, he certainly didn't have an immediate answer to every problem he faced. He was often "thinking on his feet" in the cities and communities he passed through, dealing with problems as and when they arose. Later he wrote back to the communities he had come to know, trying to respond constructively to problems that had arisen. This sense of Paul the pastor working in ever new and challenging situations is immensely important both in terms of who the historical Paul was and of the model he provides for Christian discipleship and ministry today.

Paul was a traveler and letter writer, a person who was passionate and even fanatical about his preaching and teaching. His life had been radically changed by his experience of Jesus Christ. However we deal with the problem of the relation between Paul's own letters and the Acts of the Apostles, it is clear that Paul covered a lot of ground as he founded some communities and visited others. Even though some aspects of his life might have become uncertain under the microscope of modern critical scholarship, it is still clear that Paul was a thundering type of personality whose commitment and determination seriously affected the course of early Christianity.

Though we may not be absolutely sure of details like the number of Paul's missionary journeys or whether he really studied under Gamaliel in Jerusalem, it is still clear that he had a fanatical and infectious enthusiasm that affected everyone he encountered in one way or another. Whatever Paul's relation to the historical Jesus, it is clear that his experience of the risen Christ had changed his own life beyond recognition and that he wished to communicate this good news to others. Through his writings he continued to influence Christianity down the centuries, and he still plays an important part in its teachings today.

Overall, I hope that from the essays in this book you have gained a richer sense of the real historical Paul and of the issues that arise in seriously studying his life, letters, and theology. There have been many different interpretations of both the man and his theology, but I hope that *Paul Today: Challenging Readings of Acts and the Epistles* has opened up for you new ways of approaching Paul and released him from the dusty misinterpretations that have become so common, especially at the popular level.

The "New Look" on Paul, although not accepted by all scholars, has done a great deal to release him from the theology and images that have grown up around him and obscured him down the centuries. The scholarly attempts to scrape away later interpretations of Paul's theology have gone a long way toward letting the real man emerge even though there are still inevitably many different images of him. The problems of interpreting Paul won't go away, but I believe there is no going back on what has happened in recent scholarship on his life, letters, and theology. Archaeology has opened a very important door into the world of Paul. Digging up places like Ephesus has taught us a great deal about his social environment, and critical work on his letters has shown that we have all too often read more into his writings than out of them. Scholars will continue to disagree about the big picture where Paul is concerned and about the fine detail, but it is clear that a new Paul has now emerged and I hope that you have found something of him in these pages.

As you have seen, Paul had quite different attitudes to things from the ones usually associated with him. For example, his teaching about marriage and divorce isn't just a matter of him disapproving of both things and preferring everyone to remain single as he did. His comment, "It is well for them to remain single as I do" (1 Cor. 7:8), is not an all-time ethical ruling about sex and relationships; it is much more specific to the circumstances in which he was writing. The eschatological context of his words must be taken into account if their real meaning is to emerge. Paul's attitude to slavery must also be read in the light of the eschatological expectations of the first century CE and not in the light of the nineteenth-century slave trade in Europe and the United States. The things Paul has to say about some of the other matters he faced may seem a long way from the experience of most modern readers, but his words still raise important issues for us now. So, for example, his comments about food sacrificed to idols raise questions about conscience and community that are still of importance today.

More topical still, Paul's attitudes to women and homosexuality are rather different from what is commonly imagined. A lot of people think Paul's views on these subjects are crystal clear and negative, simply waiting in his letters to be found and quoted. But once again the situation is much more complex. Paul's very words have often been used to support ideas I am sure he never had. So, when he makes comments about women wearing veils or speaking in church I am convinced that if we consider the full historical context as far as it can be discerned, we will hear a very different message. A wider consideration of the place of women in Paul's life and theology does not support the idea that he "hated women" as many people seem to think.

So with homosexuality: it is frequently maintained that Paul "condemned homosexuality." But as I have tried to show, he probably never even knew of the sort of "homosexuality" that is usually the subject of modern debates on this subject, and in any case there was no single word for it in any of the languages he knew. Again, it is a matter of taking Paul's historical context seriously, and if we are determined to find out what he really thought we must work hard at reconstructing that original context.

Similar things can be said about Paul's more explicitly theological thinking. The connections in his theology between Christ, ethics, and the church have often been obscured, and his teaching on the Fall, Original Sin, and Justification, as complex as it is, has now been shown to need a different approach. In general the task is one of removing centuries of later interpretation in order to let the real Paul emerge. As I hope you have found in these essays, this can be done without diluting the theological significance of what Paul said and its continuing importance for us today.

Finally, I hope that these *Paul Today: Challenging Readings of Acts and the Epistles* has indeed challenged your presuppositions about the famous Apostle to the Gentiles and stimulated you to further inquiries into his life, letters, and theology. Paul himself is a challenging figure, and it is important to keep reading his words over and over, interpreting them afresh in and for each new situation.

BIBLIOGRAPHY

GENERAL SOURCES

Introductions

Brown, Raymond E. *Introduction to the New Testament.* New York: Doubleday, 1997.

Johnson, Luke Timothy. *The Writings of the New Testament: An Interpretation.* Revised Edition Plus CD-ROM of Full Text and Study Tools. Minneapolis: Augsburg Fortress, 2002.

Ehrman, Bart D. *The New Testament: An Historical Introduction to the Early Christian Writings.* Oxford: Oxford University Press, 2003.

Dictionaries

Coggins, R. J. and J. L. Houlden (eds.). *A Dictionary of Biblical Interpretation.* London: SCM, 1990.

Freedman, David Noel (ed.). *The Anchor Bible Dictionary.* New York: Doubleday, 1992, six volumes.

Metzger, Bruce M. and Michael D. Coogan. *The Oxford Companion to the Bible.* Oxford: Oxford University Press, 1993.

Commentary

Barton, John and John Muddiman (eds.). *The Oxford Bible Commentary.* Oxford: Oxford University Press, 2001. Also available on CD-ROM.

Books on Paul

Crossan, John Dominic and Jonathan L. Reed. *In Search of Paul: How Jesus's Apostle Opposed Rome's Empire with God's Kingdom. A New Vision of Paul's Words and World.* New York: HarperCollins, 2004.

Dunn, James D. G. *The Cambridge Companion to St. Paul*. Cambridge: Cambridge University Press, 2003.

Dunn, James D. G. *The Theology of Paul the Apostle*. Edinburgh: T&T Clark, 1998.

Hooker, Morna D. *Paul: A Short Introduction*. Oxford: Oneworld, 2003.

Murphy-O'Connor, Jerome. *Paul: His Story*. Oxford: Oxford University Press, 2004.

Sampley, J. Paul. *Paul in the Greco-Roman World: A Handbook*. Edinburgh: T&T Clark, 2003.

Sanders, E. P. *Paul: A Very Short Introduction*. Oxford: Oxford University Press, 1991/2001.

Witherington III, Ben. *The Paul Quest: The Renewed Search for the Jew of Tarsus*. Leicester: InterVarsity, 1998.

Wright, N. T. *Paul: In Fresh Perspective*. Philadelphia: Fortress, 2006.

Ziesler, John. *Pauline Christianity*. Oxford: Oxford University Press, 1983.

Web Page

See www.ntgateway.com for a lively and comprehensive array of New Testament resources.

CHAPTER BY CHAPTER

1. A Portrait of Paul

Beker, J. Christian. *Heirs of Paul: Paul's Legacy in the New Testament and in the Church Today*. Edinburgh: T&T Clark, 1992.

Heyer, C. J. Den. *Paul: A Man of Two Worlds*. London: SCM, 2000.

Murphy-O'Connor, Jerome. *Paul: A Critical Life*. Oxford: Oxford University Press, 1996.

Pervo, Richard I. *Luke's Story of Paul*. Minneapolis: Fortress, 1990.

Roetzel, Calvin J. *Paul: A Jew on the Margins*. Louisville and London: Westminster John Knox, 2003.

Wallace, Richard and Wynne Williams. *The Three Worlds of Paul of Tarsus*. London and New York: Routledge, 1998.

2. Paul and Jesus

Bruce, F. F. *Paul and Jesus*. London: SPCK, 1977.

Furnish, Victor Paul. *Jesus According to Paul*. Cambridge: Cambridge University Press, 1993.

Hengel, Martin. *Between Jesus and Paul: Studies in the Earliest History of Christianity*. Eugene, OR: Wipf & Stock, 2003.

Matera, Frank. *New Testament Ethics: The Legacies of Jesus and Paul*. Louisville: Westminster John Knox, 1996.

Wenham, David. *Paul and Jesus: The True Story*. London: SPCK, 2002.

Witherington III, Ben. *Jesus, Paul and the End of the World: A Comparative Study in New Testament Eschatology*. Downers Grove, IL: InterVarsity, 1992.

3. Paul and Ephesus

Haenchen, Ernst. *The Acts of the Apostles: A Commentary*. Philadelphia: Westminster, 1971.

DeVries, LaMoine F. *Cities of the Biblical World*. Peabody, MA: Hendrickson, 1997.

Houlden, J. L. *Paul's Letters from Prison*. London: SCM, 1970.

Kitchen, Martin. *Ephesians*. London and New York: Routledge, 1994.

Knox, John. *Philemon among the Letters of Paul*. Chicago: 1935.

Koester, Helmut. *Ephesos, Metropolis of Asia: An Interdisciplinary Approach to Its Archaeology, Religion, and Culture.* Harvard Theological Studies. Philadelphia: Trinity Press International, 1995.

4. Contextualizing Paul

Barrett, C. K. *A Commentary on the First Epistle to the Corinthians*. London: A&C Black, 1968.

Deming, Will. *Paul on Marriage and Celibacy: The Hellenistic Background of 1 Corinthians 7*. Grand Rapids: Eerdmans, 2004.

Combes, I. A. H. *The Metaphor of Slavery in the Writings of the Early Church: From the New Testament to the Beginning of the Fifth Century*. JSNTSS, 156, Sheffield: Sheffield Academic Press, 1998.

Glancy, Jennifer A. *Slavery in Early Christianity*. Oxford: Oxford University Press, 2002.

Harrill, J. Albert. *Slaves in the New Testament: Literary, Social and Moral Dimensions*. Minneapolis: Augsburg Fortress, 2005.

Martin, Dale B. *Slavery as Salvation: The Metaphor of Slavery in Pauline Christianity*. New Haven and London: Yale University Press, 1990.

5. Discerning the Body

Cheung, Alex T. *Idol Food in Corinth: Jewish Background and Pauline Legacy*. JSNTSS, 176, Sheffield: Sheffield Academic Press, 1999.

Dunn, James D. G. *1 Corinthians*. Edinburgh: T&T Clark, 2004.

Feely-Harnik, Gillian. *The Lord's Table: The Meaning of Food in Early Judaism and Christianity*. Washington, DC: Smithsonian Institution Press, 1994.

Gooch, Peter D. *Dangerous Food: 1 Corinthians 8–10 in Its Context*. Waterloo, ON: Wilfrid Laurier University Press, 1993.

Newton, Derek. *Deity and Diet: The Dilemma of Sacrificial Food at Corinth*. JSNTSS, 169, Sheffield: Sheffield Academic Press, 1998.

Willis, Wendell L. *Idol Meat in Corinth: The Pauline Argument in 1 Corinthians 8 and 10*. Eugene, OR: Wipf & Stock, 2004.

6. Paul and Women

Bristow, John Temple. *What Paul Really Said about Women: An Apostle's Liberating Views on Equality in Marriage, Leadership and Love*. New York: HarperCollins, 1991.

Byrne, Brendan. *Paul and the Christian Woman*. Minneapolis: Liturgical Press, 1988.

Epp, Eldon J. *Junia: The First Woman Apostle*. Minneapolis: Augsburg Fortress, 2005.

Gillman, Florence M. *Women Who Knew Paul*. Minneapolis: Liturgical Press, 1992.

Hooker, M. D. "Authority on Her Head: An Examination of 1 Cor. XI.10," *New Testament Studies* 10 (1963–1964): 410–16.

Keener, Craig S. *Paul, Women and Wives: Marriage and Women's Ministry in the Letters of Paul*. Peabody, MA: Hendrickson, 1992.

Thurston, Bonnie. *Women in the New Testament: Questions and Commentary.* New York: Crossroad, 1998.

7. Paul and Homosexuality

Boswell, John. *Christianity, Social Tolerance, and Homosexuality: Gay People in Western Europe from the Beginning of the Christian Era to the Fourteenth Century.* Chicago and London: University of Chicago Press, 1980.

Countryman, L. William. *Dirt, Greed and Sex: Sexual Ethics in the New Testament and Their Implications for Today.* Philadelphia: Fortress, 1988.

Dover, K. J. *Greek Homosexuality.* Cambridge, MA: Harvard University Press, 1978.

Nissinen, Martti. *Homoeroticism in the Biblical World: A Historical Perspective.* Minneapolis: Fortress, 1998.

Rogers, Jack. *Jesus, The Bible and Homosexuality: Explode the Myths, Heal the Church.* Louisville: Westminster John Knox, 2006.

Scroggs, Robin. *The New Testament and Homosexuality.* Philadelphia: Fortress, 1983.

8. A Revolution in Pauline Studies

Dunn, James D. G. "The New Perspective on Paul," in James D.G. Dunn, *Jesus, Paul and the Law: Studies in Mark and Galatians.* London: SPCK, 1990.

Kim, Seyoon. *Paul and the New Perspective. Second Thoughts on the Origin of Paul's Gospel.* Grand Rapids: Eerdmans, 2002.

Koperski, Veronica. *What Are They Saying about Paul and the Law?* Mahwah, NJ: Paulist, 2001.

Sanders, E. P. *Paul and Palestinian Judaism.* London: SCM, 1977.

Stendahl, Krister. "The Apostle Paul and the Introspective Conscience of the West," in Stendahl, *Paul among Jews and Gentiles and Other Essays.* London: SCM, 1977.

Westerholm, Stephen. *Perspectives Old and New on Paul.* Grand Rapids: Eerdmans, 2003.

9. Paul and Christ

Dunn, James D. G. *Christology in the Making: An Inquiry into the Origins of the Doctrine of the Incarnation.* London: SCM, 1980.

Farley, Lawrence R. *The Prison Epistles: Philippians, Ephesians, Colossians and Philemon.* Ben Lomond, CA: Conciliar, 2003.

Freed, Edwin D. *The Apostle Paul and His Letters.* London and Oakville: Equinox, 2005.

Fitzmyer, Joseph A. "The Christological Hymn of Philippians 2.6–11," in Joseph A. Fitzmyer, *According to Paul: Studies in the Theology of the Apostle.* Mahwah, NJ: Paulist, 1993.

Hume, C. R. *Reading through Colossians and Ephesians.* London: SCM, 1998.

Martin, R. P. *Carmen Christi: Philippians ii.5–11 in Recent Interpretation and in the Setting of Early Christian Worship.* SNTSMS 4. Cambridge: Cambridge University Press, 1967.

10. The Fall and Original Sin

Barrett, C. K. *Reading Through Romans.* London: SPCK, 1977.

Cranfield, C. E. B. *Romans: A Shorter Commentary.* Edinburgh: T&T Clark, 1985.

Dunn, James D. G. *Romans* WBC 38, 2 vols. Dallas: Word, 1988.

Farley, Lawrence R. *The Epistle to the Romans: A Gospel for All.* Ben Lomond, CA: Conciliar, 2002.

Haacker, K. *The Theology of Romans.* Cambridge: Cambridge University Press, 2003.

Robinson, John A. T. *Wrestling with Romans.* London: SCM, 1979.

11. Justification by Faith?

Dunn, James D. G. *The Theology of Paul's Letter to the Galatians.* Cambridge: Cambridge University Press, 1993.

Grieb, A. Katherine. *The Story of Romans: A Narrative Defense of God's Righteousness.* Louisville and London: Westminster John Knox, 2002.

Haacker, K. *The Theology of Romans.* Cambridge: Cambridge University Press, 2003.

Hubner, Hans. *Law in Paul's Thought.* Edinburgh: T&T Clark, 1984.

McGrath, Alister. *Reformation Thought: An Introduction.* Oxford: Blackwell, 1988.

Stuhlmacher, Peter. *Revisiting Paul's Doctrine of Justification. With an Essay by Donald A. Hagner.* Downers Grove, IL: InterVarsity, 2001.

INDEX

ABOUT
THE AUTHOR

Stephen W. Need was born in Nottingham, UK. He received his Ph.D. in Systematic Theology from King's College London and has taught New Testament Studies in Chichester, Southampton, and Jerusalem. He has traveled widely in the Middle East and is currently dean of St. George's College Jerusalem.